PETER RE

Essential Reading

Selected and with an introduction by
Alan Jenkins

Secker & Warburg
London

First published in England 1986 by
Martin Secker & Warburg Limited
54 Poland Street, London W1V 3DF

British Library Cataloguing in Publication Data

Reading, Peter
Essential Reading.
I. Title   II. Jenkins, Alan
821'.914   PR6068.E27

ISBN 0–436–40988–7

Typeset by Inforum Ltd, Portsmouth
Printed in England by
Redwood Burn Ltd, Trowbridge

CONTENTS

ESSENTIAL READING: A NOTE

Two complications present themselves, in the case of Peter Reading, in addition to the usual problems of choosing from among a poet's individual collections for a 'Selected' volume. Not only is Reading an *un*usually prolific writer, and his an unusually varied body of work, but from as early as *The Prison Cell & Barrel Mystery* he has, rather more than most contemporary poets, conceived his books *as* books – wholes more or less unified by cross-references, contrasting approaches to the same themes, recurring settings, voices or 'characters' and even, lurking slyly behind the arrangement of poems, hints at a plot or the elements of one. Despite a relish for demotic speech and the effects produced by crossing it with some highly sophisticated metrical and syllabic patterns (effects at their most sustained in *Ukulele Music*, published last year), Reading is not exactly a dramatic poet; nor, despite his drawing on many of the resources of narrative prose, particularly as practised in the eighteenth and nineteenth centuries, with a strong vein of reportage and much use of 'found' material (or invention of it), is he strictly speaking a narrative one. More, perhaps, than the above suggests, Reading is an original: a poet of economical, elliptical fictions which, even when fantastic or closest to brutal caricature, retain a Dickensian kind of truth-value, give off a whiff of the real in their boldest imaginative strokes. The suggestion of the 'novel-in-verse' is one that Reading consciously works towards; as he has said, 'The concision of poetry appeals to me, but the novelist's job – big-scale serious tacklings of things, as in Dickens or Smollett – is something I try in a smaller way to get into what I do.' That ambition is most pronounced, and most startlingly fulfilled, in *Ukulele Music* and C. My selection from those two books, as from *5×5×5×5×5*, *Tom o'Bedlam's Beauties* and (to a lesser extent) from all the other books, attempts to do justice to as many of the interwoven voices and narrative strands as possible without sacrificing an overall continuity – this has meant retaining more of the 'dramatic' Reading at the expense, perhaps, of poems apparently spoken in the poet's own persona – and tone. As to that tone, or the charge which Reading's increasingly gruesome subject-matter, his detachment and black-comedian's sense of the grotesque have now and again incurred – the charge of heartlessness or a merely playful desire to shock – Reading has remarked: 'Art has always struck me most when it was to do with coping with things, hard things, things that are difficult to take. If you want art to be like Ovaltine, then clearly some artists are not for you.'

Inevitably, some striking and inventive poems have been left out; and no selection could fully convey the intricate design which plays a large part in making the last three or four books so exciting. But it is my hope that anyone coming to these selected poems who has not previously encountered Reading's dark, often appalled and appalling vision, his contempt for cant, 'wrong-headed duff gen' and poetry that refuses to face up to grim realities, the irony and complex, self-accusing sense of compassion and impotence he brings to bear on them, his quirky intelligence, erudition and robust humour in detailing the ways of *H. sap.*, and the vigour and ingenuity with which all these are expressed, will find not only this book but all his books essential reading.

ALAN JENKINS

From FOR THE MUNICIPALITY'S ELDERLY

Embarkation

Something today evokes (it may just be
the smell the grass makes stewing in the heat,
the sun illuminating crevices
I had not dreamed all winter still existed,
or possibly that undefined misgiving
I felt then and feel always underneath
the merely surface-pleasure summer brings –
a sense of somehow growing over-ripe)
a summer ending and a country halt.

Those in the sulphurous carriage were the same
as those who go unknown to business daily,
walk always clockwise aimless round the deck
until the plank is lowered and they file
into that city, on the other side,
of smoke and pimpled dummies and debris.
Odysseuses bound daily to commute
with rolled umbrella brief-case and dark suit.
And I have been among them on the quay,
placed pennies, at the turnstile, on our tongues.
I joined the train of lobster-pink old age.
Weeds prised the platform, where you waved, oblique.
The day was hot and stewed grass filled our lungs.

Plague Graves

We knew nothing of their existence before
you shewed us the other day five wrinkled
knobbly old and enormous fingers
tied down with heather roots tight to the moor;
and they, being buried three hundred years
ago, knew nothing about us, but neither
party's existence was any way less
for the other's ignorance of it.

                          To see
the same future waiting and still to continue
seems our most noble attribute, though
I suppose we secretly hope for some permanent
monument left of us, some recognition
by those coming after. No chance. Sheep maul
beyond recognition alarmingly quickly
the sandwich-paper memorials left
by charabanc trippers, dissolving all tangible
trace of us.

                    When the world ends and space-age
picnickers freeze to flint or melt or
asphyxiate or simply, no longer able
to read the already eroding incision,
just think five slabs have rather aesthetically
fallen above Gorse Hill, the result will
undoubtedly be the same in the final
analysis – no one to know them, extol them
or give them permanence in the now prevalent
sense of fame; and their mark will be not
in palpable stone but that they were once,
walked here, and did wonderful things.

For the Municipality's Elderly

Things here grow old and worn with untragic
logic.

      Sated we drowse supine
on a bench incised For the Municipality's
Elderly.

        Withering limbs a long summer
smoulders in ashes.

           At evensong
spent faces from almshouse windows follow us
into the dusty column of late
afternoon oblique amber. Still there persists
a smile of attained appeasement in worn
grained skulls, streaked knobs of warm butter with no more
of life left in them, misericords.

Stubble is parched on a tumulus now
that when ripe was moist peach flesh. On top of us
coiffures of willowherb fleece puff their last
uphill.

        In Castle Gardens fermenting
mulch in September, honey fumes throb
a mirage of clipped lobelia beds
where we loll and, ungrudgingly, limp with stooks
too long left on fields beyond Broad Street, brown
and burn out.

Easter Letter

Palms are down on the chancel slabs,
hope for the dead is the week after next.

The castle gleams like roasting duck,
south-facing corners irradiate
nine hundred years. Forty or so
generations like us who have willingly
browned, flaked-dry here, steam from the walls
and nettled moat.

                In a month May Fair
will occupy Castle Square, but generate
only a sense of pending departure;
relics of sympathetic men
more palpably are distilled from this
angle of sun-douched Norman stone.

I fade through years to a fair with a schoolfriend,
quite beyond contact now, the Big Wheel
sickeningly revolves, we first glimpse
immortality – our insides
keep going for ever after our bodies
have stopped.

              A more terrestrial kind
of ghostliness than Easter means
I still believe in, different from
the declaration on the plaque
BY.ADAM.IN.TE.DVST.ILYE.
BY.CHRIST.I.AVE.TE.VICTORY.

Another irony, another
season; new flowers are in the font
and on new graves.

                              The Almshouse inmate,
paralysed, is flyblown; blind
eyes from another life ascend
the dark tower of St. Lawrence's.
Bats like black balloons released,
out of control, deflating, catch
aphids newly hatched to gorge
on the uncovered corpse. The hide
is worn-transparent, stretched-tight membrane
over frail bones against the moon.

Conveniently adjacent is
the Cottage Hospital. Three weeks
I have watched the patient in
the first floor left hand window, as
at evening I return from work,
jacked-up prepared for visiting-hour.
Kleenex, hyacinth, Lucozade
are still apparent, the bed is bare,
crisp sheets are neatly creased oblique.

Turn the switch, join in the chorus
'what to do about it? – let's
put out the light and go to sleep.'

The Crucifix is now in High Street.

Spare us, good Lord, spare thy people
whom thou'st redeemed with thy most precious
blood, cried Solomon Eagle running
loose denouncing of judgement on
the City, in most frightful manner –
a pan of burning charcoal upon
his head, for the rest quite naked – through
White Chapel (1665
during another plague).

                    On short wave
the Budget fizzles out to music
interference, ritardando,
pound in the pocket pound in the grave,
reduced death duty, ritornello.

The phone's still warm from some late caller
joined now with the flickering shadows
of other evening commuters returning,
tenuous, quiet, the other side
of the glass.

                The evidence of men
vanished is thick in Deepwood Lane;
the hedge is split and pleached neat by
a ghost. No-one remembers who
installed the boozey where beasts schnorkel
sweet molassed oat straw.

                    A crust
of lichen seals the lid on a former
curate of Pipe Aston under
his favourite yew. The list of vicars
since the church was built has filled
only one quarto sheet, congregations
are still here mulched in the cider orchard.

With apparatus for rolling and raising
heavy objects, a fat man in tails
converses with matron, opens the boot.

Eli, Eli, lama sabachthani?

Faithful and simpleton are singing
hope for the dead from this morning on.
Wipe the dust from the chocolate egg.
A human hip bone stirs on the pile
of strewn daffs in the Garden of Rest.

Juncture

Where I work, a rural siding
breaks from the northern/southern route,
provides a parsleyed cul-de-sac
narrow-gaúge alternative.

So strange to see you, whom I loved
ten years ago, flicker across
the gap in this abandoned cut
with red No Smoking triangles,
my still not-quite-extinguished flame,
with unmistakable reflex
shifting hair from brow to temple.

Spring has returned to me; you can't.

The life I led in your world, now
seems the slow death of someone else.
Memory returns without me.
Are you receiving me through steel
dolorous Inter-City lines?

Are my contemporaries dead?
Has drink or pot claimed Pom. and Baz.?
Mad Dawson who once shaved his head
rather than lose a ten bob bet –
severed, that pate recurs in dreams,
black puckered walnut soused in brine.
Mooj. with his eighth-rate lectureship,
rearguarding what new Ism? You
drowned when your scallop shell capsized
only last night in warm white-fleeced
Aegean, and I woke up stiff.

Decaying here at least is lush.
Stinkhorn festers each side of me,
parsnip wine last Christmas gave me
shrunk-tight granny-knot intestines.
We kill rats with crab-tree sticks,
we thread jackdaws on a blackthorn,
spike dead moles like finger-stalls.
Teddy is lynched on next door's line.

Wallflowers drench the air with syrup –
I recall St. Philip's Garden
from the arched gate where it started,
coupled with a sad misgiving
that, whereas you never loved me
while I loved you, you might love me
after I had ceased to love you.

There you buried that world for me,
and its unreal population;
now your unexplained appearance
from the window of a train
at this distant country juncture
leaves behind a trail of sleepers
drawn out from infinity.

Combine

Being neutral, the first we see of it is its shadow
approaching, laying bare whole acres.
                                        The vast
departure is now irrevocably underway;
only telegraph wires are alive, the sky is empty.

Sap sinks from live limbs, the dead are shrouded with mauve
faeces of birds gorged sick on blackberries.

I seem to have been with you only an instant here;
idyllic becomes fearful grave silence as I awake
to you already arisen, the steady thresh
and much nearer shadow of the quiet harvester.

Burning Stubble

All stubble is being burned, a chiffon pall
is settling over round flesh-tint hills, it seems haunches
of supine bodies unbreathing after a fall.

We see them for the last time, all those men, their huge
efficient harvest; last light is pressing the panes.

Off the Teme at this season fog sinks us all, snuffs each
light in the low water-meadow out.

                       We have grown
to expect these things here at this time (late harvest),
pyres, the extinguishing suck of mists
on September dusks, as we expect
winter thrushes in season and
the dark swift coming and going.

Night-Piece

Although ready to, I can't get to sleep yet,
detained by forty huntsmen galloping
all dressed black up an unfamiliar
lane, or clocking a ton in a sports job
steered by the wife of a friend. I sweat
curry powder, events of the day are reduced
to clipped rushes . . . off goes the Sprite with the blonde
whom I kiss goodnight as if for the last time.

We sit facing west towards evening, watch
England grow dark and disappear, swallow
two more finos and draw the curtains.
And then one more, to make up for lost time.

Ball claps bat. We're aware today
of perhaps our only achievement ever –
carrying on as if nothing was wrong (though
I kiss you tonight as if for the last time).

Turned earth, the empty trench, then we enter
among varicose alabaster knights
and petrified other Elizabethans.
The Great G minor Fantasia
knits an acoustic cobweb; however
curtains refuse to reveal the player
playing tonight as if for the last time.

Even our best friends' three-year-old daughter,
an Armageddon of pink ice-cream,
reminds me that there are too many of us.
Kiss her tonight as if for the last time.

Black in the face, gasping fish-out-of-water,
white palmed, white rim round mouth, baby gulps
Al-Jolson-like (Mammy Mammy Mammy,
a million miles for your smiles for the last time).

Latest computer forecasts inform us
in thirty years time she'll be gulping for real.
Top-up your larynx before they call Time Please.

The modern finale is molto vivace
. . . a pause . . . across fields to the chancel wafts
applause, a good man is run-out at thirty.
Pick up his stump, hang it up for the last time.

Under the curtain the unrevealed player
(volles werk volles werk spun and woven)
cuts to a weird choreography done
by Clotho, Lachesis, Atropos,
circling the bed in infectious ragtime.

From THE PRISON CELL & BARREL MYSTERY

Early Stuff

I have been looking through his early stuff.

'You have' he wrote of me in 'Poster Girl'
'the same too good to touch, too high to reach
qualities as that ad. girl, quite too much
to hope for. Your blouse wrinkles in the rain,
and where your heart is, underneath the now
transparent pink silk, re-appears the man
who you were stuck on last.'

                                    In his 'Au Pair'
'My now bare moon-beamed room is claustrophobic,
along the shore the last ebb churns. Tonight
I kiss your thin hand noting the blue vein
of Biro slowly crinkling in my hold
as I release burnt fragments to the reflux
leaving moist shale, an empty shell, and ash
of what you wrote unlovingly from France.'
That was unfair.
                    We parted shortly after.

'A new-sawn stack of peeling birch fence poles
at ithyphallic 45 degrees
unheals a year's scar, resurrects this scene:
the sun streaming through branches in thin lines
pierces with shadows soft as velvet moles
the rind peeled back on piled lopped logs of birch,
a girl's hair deep and smelling of coal tar
shadows my face again. The sun is low.
Our shadows now are longer than we are.'
After 'Umbrae' we patched things up.

'Re-linked
in the park palmhouse hot glass cranium,
temperature rises with each opening door,
tormented steamy ferns drip, your tights stick,
air clings to lungs like candyfloss. Outside
lovers are strewn like white stones on the banks
of the brown lake. I wither for your love.
It is as hot as Hell – ironically
this globe sustains a Bird of Paradise.'

Of course he cashed in when Grandmother died
'The quack says there's no chance, meanwhile she sleeps.
The sloppy Indiarubber line-rimmed mouth
sags closed, you have to poke it with the fork
to make it open when you whisper "food".
Poke poke poke poke – tonight it's closed for keeps'.

The affair was at its height in 'Cemetery',
'She lies aslant a lettered slab unmoved,
stone Virgin newly down from the white plinth.
Because of Her, roots spring from graves cracked open
by Her descent. The love that makes bones live
moves even here warmed by her marble hand.'
Quite nice.

But he could have his nasty side,
e.g. 'Misprint in Last Year's Horoscope'
(he was a Leo, me a Capricorn)
'That crap about a deep relationship
with, of all things, a Leo, was quite wrong.
It should have been: *avoid* Leos, they're losers,
they've no virility, they're bloody fairies,
they end up in the Arts or in the boozers.
You need a ram, a young ram, try an Aries.'

Or 'Caricature Angel', 'Christmas Eve,
I have strung up the Magi, Santa Claus,
Rudolph the Red-nosed Reindeer, Jesus Christ,
shepherds astonished, snowman with a pipe,
a perky robin. What I need most now
is a Madonna. Thumbing through the pile
of cards, I find a caricature angel
(signed, and with kisses now quite meaningless)
straddling in kinky boots an awed adorer.'

He seems not to have known I loved him then
(he married someone else) but found out later.

Nocturne

Two concurrently are dreaming

I have got your
still warm ashes
in a plastic
carrier bag
fastened to my
palm with three inch
self-tap chrome screws
which a former
lover tries to
free but can't turn
anticlockwise

we have quarrelled
and you leave me
without kissing
me goodbye but
three months later
I ascend the
attic stairs to
find you brittle
unforgiven
beard meshed tight with
silver cobwebs

and wake up with night before them
each observing in the other's
pupil the familiar brightness
undimmed though a bloom reflects new
dark beyond the present bedroom.

Trio

Alcohol, night attire.	What is her nightie like? What sort of underclothes?	He used to recommend books for me. That was ten years ago. Each night he reads to her; I'd like that.
In her eyes almost love ten years since ankle deep acer leaves and lime hearts sapless, crushed.	Whispers he loves me, but what makes him love her still?	Whispered he loved me still, O.K. why marry her?
Would she still willingly love me now?	Would she be, has she been, willingly screwed by him?	Do they think I'd still be willingly loved by him?
On last year's Christmas card I, restrained, wrote are you happy/well?	Her letters' reticence – does she think he does not want me to know she writes?	On last year's Christmas card I, restrained, answered no I'm not/not.

Extension
three three three

He may be
even now
ringing her.

I'm in town
for a week.

I shall be
occupied
each night till
half past nine
(that's the time
my, you know,
has to get
back to his
wife and kids)
That's all right   sorry I
quite O.K.
can't be helped
never mind.

How about
Saturday?

lovely. Look
forward to
seeing you.

Lovely. CLICK.

8 a.m.
Saturday
he leaves his
hotel room,
baths, Vosene
egg protein
hair shampoos,
by the glass
squeezes spots,
checks his tie
and departs.

Ferry, bus,
he descends.
Buys from a
florist mixed
daffodils/
irises.

He reads the
doors aloud
61
63
65
next one's hers
69.

One hundred
miles away
she's alone,
sleeps. Upstairs
hangs a drawn
pencil corpse
portrait of
him who now
distantly
checks his tie
and departs.

10 a.m.
Weetabix.
He's away
for a week
she tells her
coffee cup.

He's away
for a week
she tells the
unmade bed.

She awakes
does her face,
greens her eyes,
pouts, descends,
Maxwell House,
Radio 2.

Buys avo-
cado pears,
Brie, courgettes,
Burgundy,
chicken from
Sainsburys.

12, she is
Hoovering,
door bell rings.

One thing I
never liked
was her hair.

Is the Brie
over-ripe?
Is the Beaune
good enough?

Will he make
rude remarks
– we had an
argument
once, about
wall to wall
carpeting.

One dozen
irises
one dozen
daffodils.

He'll be now
at her door.

What sort of
house is it?
What sort of
furniture?
What sort of
kitchen and
bathroom and
bedroom suite?

By the way,
Diana
sends her love.

All very
middle class
all very
aimez-vous
Mon Repos?

Does she still
have long dark
lovely hair?

In your eyes
almost grief.
Tell me now.

He must have
been there now
several hours.

She could have
got him once
easily.

First there was
you who I
deeply loved
when too late.
Fill your glass.

Are they drunk?

Her marriage
soon went flat.

Then him I
married who
I thought I
loved enough.
Have some more?

If they get
drunk she may. . .

He said she's
hooked on a
married man,

Now when I
am in love
he is a
married man.

some people
court bad luck.
In vino
veritas
I'm afraid
for them both.

Funny how
things turn out.
Encore Beaune?

I loved her
very much,
and still do.
Not to say
that in my
loving her
I was not
deeply in
love with you,
and still am.

Solo now
I sing flat:
youth must with
age decay
beauty will
fade away
castles are
sacked in war
chieftains are
scattered far
love is a
fixèd star
ha ha ha
ha ha ha.

When Puss dies
I'll be lost.
Your eyes are
very blue.
I'm afraid
to grow old.
I wouldn't
have T.V.
but for the
loneliness.
Why did you
marry her?

He now leaves
69
takes her arm.

Bus arrives
he boards bus
drops fare in
plastic bowl
waves to her
watching him
from the stop,
bus departs.

6.40
of the whole
two dozen
passengers
he looks most
lachrymose.

6 p.m.
she prepares
one boiled egg.

Slices toast
in thin strips

dips them in
absently.

Takes his arm
at the door.

Bus station
6.30
she gazes
into his
eyes, he waves,
she waves back,
him from bus
her from stop,
bus departs

she appears
sadder than
anyone
else in sight.

8 at night
Saturday.
Dines with friends,
too much Krug
with hors-d'oeuvres
too much Bual
with dessert.

10 p.m.
Saturday
he 'phones up:
nosh wish to
trude introo
simly a
soshul call
no wish trude
no wish tall
nottot tall
nottot at
losh love losh
love losh love.

Past midnight.
Unconscious.

V.H.F.
Saturday
evening play:
TIME present
SCENE bedroom
sensual
whisperings
(modern stuff).

What are they
doing now?

Trusting his
love she sleeps
– cellular
warmth of bed.

Hurls empties
into bin.
Sniffs vase of
flowers, smiles,
sits alone
with T.V.

She answers
telephone:
love you're drunk

goodnight love.

Insular,
wrapped in white
glacial sheets.

How was she?

What have I
done? Why me?
(Love me, love
my black cat.)

I loved him
but too late
(love me, love
my black cat).

My husband
I disliked
(love me, love
my black cat).

I love a
married man
(love me, love
my black cat).

Can't things go
right just once?
(Love me, love
my black cat.)

Now in the
women's ward
uterus
near defunct
(love me, love
Seemed O.K.   my black cat).

27

Correspondence

Dear Martin,
                    Bumped into Arthur tonight
(after a concert of, can you guess?
Sibelius – do you remember how
you and I loved his 2nd and 7th?)
and we got talking somehow about you.
I'm back here now. I had to write to you.
My marriage turned out a bit of a mess.
How are you? Drop me a line,
                              Love,
                                    Heather.

Dear Heather,
                    Just a note to thank you for
writing. My marriage has broken up. Karen
has gone to live in a caravan with
a Welsh self-taught painter who recently
got a grant from the Welsh Arts Council to make
a cartoon film. She took the child with her.
I'm living here at the house and would like
to see you if you could make it,
                              Love,
                                    Martin.

Dear Clive,
                    Just a few lines to tell you the
score. My marriage has broken up. Karen
has gone to live in a caravan with
a Welsh self-taught painter who recently
got a grant from the Welsh Arts Council to make
a cartoon film. She took the child with her.
I'm living here at the house with a girl
called Heather,
                    Hope to see you soon,
                                    Mart.

28

Dear Clive,
            I came across Arthur the other
night. (I'd been to a concert of Symphonies
2 and 7 by Sibelius
– thought of those 78s you bought me!)
Somehow we started talking about you.
Marriage for Martin and me was a mess.
I went to live with an artist – but now . . . well,
never mind. Drop me a line,
                        Love,
                              Karen.

Dear Karen,
            I'm on my own again now.
Me and Heather have parted company.
I feel sorry about it – lonely
and sad would be more accurate. But
I couldn't live with her any more
I'm afraid. I feel I've sort of betrayed her
– and now I think I prefer being hurt to
hurting someone else,
                        All the best,
                              Martin.

Dear Karen,
            Just a short note to say thanks for
writing. I'd heard from Mart that you'd broken up.
Sorry to hear it – you know I was always
very very fond of you. I should've
liked to invite you over some time but, well,
it's a bit awkward to tell you the truth, I'm
sort of involved with someone called Heather – look,
why not come over and see us *both*?
                        Love,
                              Clive.

The Prison Cell & Barrel Mystery

Asked to set the table

incongruously I find myself
suddenly in the chilled garden at dusk
distracted perhaps by two I passed earlier
pressed close extracting more than usual
savour from kissing – the line of the girl's
cheek so reproduced yours that personae
and time shifted.

        Your brittle account of
marriage to someone else as 'a bit
of a mess' rustles now again from tremulous
leaves.

        I am outside.

        Through glass the warm hearth.

Fleetingly trodden thyme shrouds me bruised
irredeemably under my own weight.

        *

In a glass catafalque he
eyes the black receiver, lips
set, soundproofed fingers drum
the double beat and pause of
a ringing call unanswered

one minute elapses

a young woman approaches,
suddenly recognizes
him within, audibly
inhales, taps the glass twice

'you're just the same' indicates
they have not met for some time,

as if resurrected
he emerges, hands join
familiar as old
well made dovetails.

*

Anthracite seams prise open, gush.
You re-kindle your flat fire.
Panes bloom, admit only dark now.

Remember from under ground
(wormwood, Shadows, The 'Stones)
ascending into a city
drenched in sun, embracing?

You whisper what I have not known
until now – only reticence
caused you to turn away then.

Sealed for these aeons in dark
vegetal pressure, a breath bursts,
ignites, unshadows your temple.

*

I have worn this jacket a decade; its first
night out you deposited a dark copper
hair on the shoulder which I kept
in a page of La Vita Nuova where
it still is. Tonight you implant another
mysteriously under the heart where
a week from now I am to discover it
scarcely less lustrous than at first.

*

Awaking to your
holding my head
and a glass to my lips
I thought a system of
converse ironies
in operation
and we after all
were together.

The cold
that struck my bowels then
was at her absence
– changing to grief at
recalling how fleeting
is this our reunion.

I have not seen you
for so long now that
you count as a corpse.

Already you dress
put black on your eyes
to cross the river
again for the city.

*

Your number is being rung
I request your extension

shall we meet again tonight
I return tomorrow

I shall wait anyway
meet me there if you possibly can

meet me there if you possibly can
meet me there if you poss

the line's down speak up
I am crossed with a man in the corn trade

buying Number Three Corn
ex the S.S. Arrivederci.

                              *

The Post House almost unchanged – our table
occupies the same place on the stairs,
mahogany Bacchus impartially
glares from a cluster of maturer vintage,

The Change Up and The Change Down are not
evident now, but a pleasant vignette
of what the old place was is rooted
still in these walls, a Music Hall playbill
revives THE OLD SPECTACULAR,

                              regulars
seem the same though most might tell you
of ten years' ironies almost to match
our own.

          Gone ten . . .

                    you won't make it now. . .

'licensed hours is licensed hours sir!'. . .

again tonight after ten years, unchanged,
we still pursue separate double ironies. . .

ghosts of THE GREATEST SHOW IN THE WORLD,
THE WINNERS OF THE GREAT HANDCUFFS CONTEST,
THE PRISON CELL & BARREL MYSTERY.

Duologues

1.

'Whabout that piece as lives on the farm
you delivers to, Stokey? Er as you fancies?
Up-over somewheres, Furrow Ill is it? Or
Mount Flirt or Stonewall Ill or The Warren?'

                                        'Oh,
you means er out Boultibrooke way. I
knowed er long afore ever I come
to drive for South Shropshire Farmers. Well,
er inna bad lookin mind, just one thing
– they reckons as ers a bit loony like. See,
er bloke (im as ad that motor bike crack
comin ome off the piss that time Gonder's Neck way)
e got buried in Boultibrooke churchyard
as lies at back of the farmuss, so
as er looks out er bedroom er sees is stone and
they reckons as ow er throws fits and falls
in a ruck evertime er thinks on it.'

2.

'That piece as Vaughany were toppin an tailin,
us inna sid er for a bit – er as served
at the King's Arms.'

'Ers jed a cancer, mon, died,
oh, months since. Er was in Ludlow ospital
weeks – course old Vaughany couldna go visit er,
account of er usband were allus there, so
e rings up Matron everday, asks
ow er is. Course old Matron wants to know
oo e is – e says as ees makin enquiries
for a friend of ers in Ereford. Well,
when Matron tells er as an Ereford friend
sends love to er, er knowed well enough then
it was Vaughany – see they'd arranged it previous.
After a bit mind, er old brain gets fuddled like
(er went stiff a day or two after) and
er says to Matron "what friend in Ereford?"
So nex time e rings, Matron asks old Vaughany
"what's the name of this Ereford friend?" Well,
never a flicker mind, Vaughany says "Alice
as works in Woolworths in Ereford." Thats
the last as ever e ad to do with er.'

3.

'I wish I'd knowed im as drives tractor, afore I wed Jim.
Once you marries the wrong un youm never the same someow.'

'Same along o me, Annie, that un as I fancied first,
e never said much all them years as us was courtin,
so I thinks as e dunna like me, an breaks up with im.
Then e thinks as I dunna like im, an takes some wench else.
Then I sid im again, one Pig Day it were in the Arms,
and e says as e loves me an would I get wed to im
(only would I answer im quick or eed af to wed er).
Well, I never says "ar" nor "no" for days, till e thinks
as it's "no" and e weds this other out Clungunford way
an they moves down Tenbury country – Glebe Farm an summat.

An e dunna get on with er, an just now e writes me
as e loves me, an I writes back as I loves im an all.
Just now all is stock dies – that Foot and Mouth year afore last –
and they says as e got debts an that's why e shot isself.'

Ménage à Trois

'Make yourself coffee, and *feel* the place.'
Said the psychologist's mistress and the
psychologist's wife and the psychologist
to Michael when he arrived.

                              So he sat
in the kitchen drinking black Nescafé
while in the garden the psychologist's
mistress lay on the lawn and pretended
to read Gide from a grubby thumbed Penguin.
Over Michael in the kitchen clambered
nude and T-shirted malicious infants
(sired by the psychologist, of both his wife
and his mistress) with chocolate and phlegm
besmirching their jowls in equal amounts.

High Summer. He heard through the open door
a buzzard mew on an aloof thermal.

In the Ballroom music was playing. The
psychologist and his wife were dancing.
Strauss wafted through the open French window.

Suddenly the psychologist's mistress
leapt from the lawn, let out a loony yell,
'A*A*A*A*A*A*A*A*AGH!
WHY MUST HE TAUNT ME TAUNT ME TAUNT ME SO?!',
ran upstairs, Strauss stopped on the gramophone.
All the kiddies snivelled orchestrally.

Upstairs bounded the psychologist,
rowed with his doxy, rushed down, said 'damn, DAMN!',
jumped on a little Japanese motor bike,
revved up and roared off – brrrm brrrm brrrm brrrm.

Wife and mistress shrieked, scratched, screeched, bit, tore, spat.
Michael shouted 'you are all mad, mad, MAD!',
ran to his Renault, got in, started up,
when out rushed the wife and the mistress of
the psychologist (Michael locked his door)
and snarled through the windscreen wagging their fingers
'we may be mad, Michael, but, GOD, IT'S *REAL*.'

Gravel drive crunched, he accelerated.
Outside the gate he thought 'I must remember
this for my novel. Meanwhile I must tell
my friend Peter Reading about it – he'll
probably find it terribly funny.'

From NOTHING FOR ANYONE

*(Mercifully, we're only
molested by the Big Issue
in the watches of the night:
in daylight hours we busy
ourselves with the Trivial.)*

' "Iuppiter ex alto periuria ridet amantum" 15s 6d'

A lady's album of 1826
in my possession, contains the following.

*

Two songs – 'Dear Maid, I Love Thee (andantino)',
'Why Hast Thou Taught Me To Love Thee? (allegro)'.

*

'Dear Helen, on my life, I vow,
And 'tis a sacred token,
The friendship which unites us now,
By me, shall ne'er be broken.

(R.S. September 1826.)'

*

'Extempore Lines Addressed To Helen

If to esteem thee be a crime,
I ne'er can be forgiven;
If doomed to love thee and repine,
Be merciful, kind heaven.

(E.H. Nov. 1826 Leeds.)'

*

'Should pleasure be my future lot,
Or human cares o'ertake me,
This pledge shall never be forgot,
This heart shall not forsake thee.

(R.S. Brighton. May 1827)'

*

'CONTEMPLATION (FOR A LADY'S ALBUM)', written by
E.H. in July 1827 in Hastings, is illegible apart from two
underlined fragments:

'. . . my desolate heart . . .'

'. . . in our first, happier days . . .'

*

'EPITHALAMIUM (FOR MY BRIDE, HELEN) by E.H.
Jan. 1828, London.' is wholly illegible.

*

A contribution entitled 'Early Love – lines addressed
to a young lady from her mother' is badly foxed, and
illegible apart from the opening paragraph:

'Nothing is perhaps more dangerous to the
future happiness of women of our thoughts
and cultured habits, than the entertaining
of an early, long, and unfortunate attach-
ment . . .'

*

More songs:

'The Bride's Farewell',
'To A Faded Flower',
'Oh! No, We Never Mention Him'.

*

Illegible; then:

'With ardent flame and honest heart
I'll never cease to love thee!

R.S. (London, March 1828)'

*

'A boat at midnight sent alone
To drift upon the moonlit sea;
A wounded bird, who has but one
Imperfect wing . . .' (illegible)' . . .
Is like what I am without thee!

R.S. (Edinburgh, Jun. 1829)'

*

'Once more, enchanting girl, adieu!
I must be gone while yet I may.
Oft shall I weep to think of you,
But here I will not, cannot stay!

O could I – No! It must not be!
Adieu! A long, a long adieu!
– Yet still, methinks, you frown on me,
Or never could I fly from you!

(R.S., site of John Groot's House, Dec. 1829)'

*

'NEWINGTON BOOKSHOP
LIVERPOOL
1962'

on the endpaper. And in a cryptic academic hand:

' "Iuppiter ex alto periuria ridet amantum" 15s 6d'

On Hearing The First Cuckoo In Spring

Unbearable: (1) listening
to music any more (unless
in the safe company of others),
(2) vegetal spring stirrings –

each an insufferable glimpse,
a split-second's primal clarity,
of Not-Quite-Graspable Potential/
Dimly-Recollected Guilt.

The John o'Groats Theory

'When Alison left Gregory for Miles
Gregory went to pieces. Angela
– that's Miles's wife – was not resentful, but
she went to pieces also. As for Mark,
– that's Alison and Greg's elder boy – he
got a complex and started throwing knives.
Russell – their younger – got a nervous lisp.
Sally and Abigail – Angela's girls
by her first marriage – urinate in class
(their Headmaster says this is natural).
Penny and Gordon – Miles and Angela's
own children – are quite normal, but *will* ask
"When is our Daddy coming home again?"
Mr and Mrs Smythe – Miles's parents –
were terribly upset; they'd always said
"Miles and his wife are *so* compatible."
Angela's people took it even worse;
her mother – Esther Everoyd – has been
prostrate since hearing of it. (Mr E.
is Angela's step-father, actually.
Her father is a Mr Inkerman
who visits her still – Angela, that is –
but doesn't seem to care that they're divorced.)
The Atwells, who are Gregory's parents,
have all their work cut out trying to care
for Gregory – he's hospitalized now.
Mr and Mrs Hotchkinson, you know,
– Alison's parents – seem embarrassed more
than upset (I've a feeling they were pleased
when Alison left Gregory for Miles).'

*

'well I'm broad-minded, *but*'

                              'a bloody lout –
pardon my French'

                    'he *really* was *too* much'

'no way to treat a wife'

                         'well I've heard "language",
what with the Rugby Club and all that, *but*,
well, he was going just a bit *too* far'

'he said to Howard "You can 'eff off', too" –
in front of *women*'

                              'well I'm broad-minded, *but*'

                              *

'There are two letters – one from my sister and one from Mummy
I'll read them out to you "Dear Sue, How do you like my super new
writing paper? At least it doesn't weigh very much. I'm at Mum's
this weekend as it's Jenny's last weekend. She spent all morning
packing and left at 12.30 with Andrea and her father in their car
Richard has been staying here this weekend as well. We all had a
good time at Christmas except that Mummy caught my bug I think
and wasn't feeling too good on Boxing Day. Roger came up for New
Year and we all stayed here on Thursday and Friday. We played a lot
of games including 'Formula 1' which Jenny and Richard bough
me. We went to my flat on the Friday night as we had to try out my
new casserole dish. We made a super meal with steak and kidney
swede, onion, carrots and dumplings and we had a bottle of wine as
well. Roger brought all his stereo equipment with him so we
listened to a lot of records and played 'Formula 1'. It was the
weekend of the wind so I was glad Roger was there as he is a tower
of strength. Some of the houses lost tiles and fences but mine was
O.K. Thank you very much for the tea-cosy and stand. Both jus
what I needed of course. Now my second cup of tea isn't cold and up

till now I'd been using the whole tea-tray as a stand (also that cutting board you gave me). Pity about leaving all your presents in the Left Luggage Office, still, it sounds as if you enjoyed your return journey. I suppose you're back now at work. I must say I envy you your long holidays. Next week is Roger's Works Dinner-Dance so am looking forward to it except I'm so overweight I haven't got anything to wear. The following week is our Managers' Dinner so I don't think I'm going to lose much weight in the next fortnight. My *New Year's Resolution is to lose* 1 ½ stone before my birthday. Jenny was over 10 stone this morning so if I could lose that much I'd be lighter than her! Mummy and Daddy are in the garden cutting down trees and broken branches. One went last night outside the lounge front window. A whole tree went over at the top of the road the previous weekend pulling up a gas main. The lights were also out here for about 2 hours. We had blood collectors at work the other day so decided to go just to see what blood group I am. I remember you going when you were at Art College. Anyway the last thing I said was 'You can't faint lying down.' I now know that you can! It really was quite funny in that I didn't feel as if I was going to at all. I just did and I came back not knowing where I was. I think that's about it. Hope you didn't catch my bug when you were here. Happy New Year. Love from Debbie. P.S. Glad to hear Donald is back from his 'holiday' and hope all goes well for you both again and works this time." And the other one says "Dear Susan, Very many thanks for lovely Christmas presents. We have already enjoyed the Arthur Negus Antiques book and have found much to interest us. So far we have not sampled the crystallized fruits, but I know we will enjoy that luxury soon. Debbie has given you most of the news, I'll just add a few lines. Jenny phoned to say she had settled into the university life again, and the trip by car was O.K. On Friday evening we had a phone call from David, he was in London on his return flight to U.S.A. He had been on a business trip to the Philips plant in Holland and expects to make the trip every three months. Of course being a top man in computers means his firm looks after him very well, it is a very well paid job and very very secure. It's such a nice morning here (Tuesday) Dad and I are about to start moving soil in preparation for the new greenhouse. Daddy mowed the lawn yesterday – a little bit early in the year, I think, but it now looks very smart and it now remains for me to finish the edges. Hope you are right in taking D back like that, without a murmur – still, you know best of course. Expect you have now settled back to work routine again. Hope all goes well. Lots and lots of love, Mummy." Don't tell me you haven't been listening darling, I said "There are two letters – one from my sister and one from Mummy. I'll read them out to you 'Dear Sue, How do you like my super new writing paper? . . .' " '

*

'Shh! I want to hear this bloke on the box.'

'. . . that however close to someone you are,
however perfect and irreplaceable
seems the union, in reality
transplant yourself twenty years back anywhere –
John o' Groat's, say – and benign Biology
will lead you to love someone else and believe
you love them exclusively, so uniquely
it couldn't have happened with anyone else
anywhere else. Which is to say
we are most of us perfectly capable
of falling in love (to a fairly profound
degree) with any or all of a larger
cross-section of the opposite sex
than normal social and matrimonial
codes make it comfy to realize . . .'

'E.g. I have fallen in love with you
without falling out of love with my wife.'

Travelogue

It used to be a tiny place until
a bunch of whizz-kid architects had done
their stuff. Ten dozen brash unfinished cheap.
concrete and warped pine cantilevered lumps
of arty-farty blocks and nick-nack shops
await completion for the winter takings.

But now it's August and it's pissing down.
Construction gangs are rained-off, ski-lifts drip,
hotels are all FERMETURE ANNUELLE,
La Place de Jeunesse is portcullised shut,
dust rests on skiing tanned shop-window dummies,
board pavements echo, you can't get a drink.

A child spoons from a damp pile left by builders
grey wet grit on the head of his drenched puppy.
Marooned, a stone-built shack (hens on dirt floor)
and a bewildered oldie – the only one
dourly expecting *not* to show a profit
after this winter's sport at Les Deux Alpes.

*

Menton, on the Med.
Elsewhere, honest autumn.
Here, summer dwindles.
Crones crawl through hurled swash –
Gandhis, Oxfam ads.
Perky young firm bums
and tits grow over-ripe.
Olives darken, fill,
fall on the Tende road.
Once Clicquot was swigged
from their sweet slippers.
Cheap plastic flip-flops,
Labyrinth soles.
Cattle-trucks rev on
the prom, take veal
for the abattoir. Like
a bloodhound's eyes,
flab droops. The breeze
is edged with salt;
tiers of near-dead
leaves shiver, turn
backs on the low sun.

*

In the Château d'Antibes, Musée Picasso:
polyglot coach-hordes reverentially
cluster ten deep and peer at, from two inches,
doodles, framed opulently in wrought gilt,
which (in Italian, French, German and English)
a Guide tries desperately to justify.
'This is a Post-Synthetic Cubist work.
Poseidon *with his trident* is a symbol.
Here, *Form* and *Image* matter more than *Likeness*.'
(Vague crap, the sort they tell you on Pre-Dip.)
Perplexed suburban mums, despairing fraus,
middle-aged middle-class Europe huddles up
united in its mutual dazed wonder

at how an alien culture could creep on
and overtake it in its own lifetime.
A dozen Japs behind Yashikas enter,
grinning incredulous bewilderment.
Twelve flashes (doubtless for projection later
in front of supercilious Tokyo smirks).
The oldest has a young girl at his side
(who holds hands with an English-looking bloke)
and scrutinizes marks where paint has drooled,
then whispers to her. Bright gold fillings glint.
'Grandfather say of Art of East and West
"Sometimes is interesting, sometimes a puzzle,
sometimes is" – how the English say? – "slipshod." '

*

Camping Provençal. Notices: (1)
Tourists may only settle in the camp,
after if having checked in at the office
they know their places. (2) The campers' dresses
must be correct in camp. (3) Please no noise
between the 22 and seven-o-clock.
(4) In the camp, parents must watch across
their children. (5) Take care of the plantations,
don't set up nails nor pour dish-water on
the trees. (6) Fire-woods are forbidden. (7)
Linen must dry discretely. (8) Detritus,
put this into the dustbins. (9) Showers-bath,
wash-house and W.C. must be kept clean.
Water is quite uncommon in Provence.
(10) Management is NOT responsible
for thefts. (11) Speed don't exceed 5.
(12) *That* box is reserved alone for throw
sanitary-towels and periodicals.
(13) These rules must be respected under
penalty of your time expiring here.

*

When I went it was Saturday. Les Grottes
de Niaux are Sunday-opening. A tight
steel door, as to a bank vault, locked away
graffiti twenty thousand years (approx)
of age. But I had seen it on a carte
postale illustrée – bison speared, vague blot
of antelope*. Quite fascinating? Yes,
because of something other than good art.

A Zeppelin dick in felt-tip stains the rocks.

To aid the hunt? To work off horniness?
Partly, no doubt. And partly both convey,
and partly were inspired by, mortal fright.

*

This is where Bernadette
visioned the Virgin and wet
     herself (1858)
     and the distempered congregate –
Iron Lungs, Kidney Machines, crutches –
confidently, for such is
     the miraculous property of the Spring
     that a few swigs cure anything
(with the notable omission
of Catholic superstition).

* I have subsequently learned that wild horses, not
antelopes, feature in the cave paintings at Niaux.

Concrete is glib, gleams with generations
of pilgrims' melted candle-wax which
Municipal workers scrape up. A nutter
caresses the cave wall, gives it French kisses.
Multi-lingual Masses every
15 minutes. Nick-nack emporia –
plastic bottles for the magic water,
3D cards of the grotte. From the rock
crutches dangle, Maria simpers.
Factory girls as they pass get down
on the knees of torn tights, kiss tarmac (icy
at 8 a.m.). The afflicted amass.
Rosary-fumbling parents of
a child who is (predictably, since
they must have been over 40 when
the happy event took place) a Mongol.
Precocious of me, I know, but: 'Irreverence
is a greater oaf than Superstition'?,
W.H.A., *really*!

Nothing For Anyone

Cancel our Dailies and Monthlies.

Population, Energy, Food.
The present United Nations
Forecast of Population
for year 2000 is over
7,000 millions.
Lord Ashby spells it out for us*
(*Encounter*, March 76) –
for Western Industrial Man
this isn't just another
crisis but a climacteric.

Less weighty, a Sunday Sup.
reports on Alcoholism.

The Art Correspondent, clearly,
don't know his Arp from his Albers.

In Essex, I read, there are more
ponies per square stockbroker's
daughter than anywhere else.

This sot's liver – a metaphor
for sterling's swollen decease
and Technological Man
and before him Roman, Mayan,
Minoan, all *Homo erectus*
and what he conceives as Cosmos
in his own petty perspective
blown oversize by an ego
too big to survive itself.

* *A Second Look at Doom, by Eric Ashby, Encounter, Vol XLVI No. 3*

(What else but dummies like us
could aim for 'More motor cars
to put us back on our feet'?)

Some snivelling Celt reviews verse.
Compared with De Witts' Black Holes,*
a handful of weighed syllables
has no future (nor has future).

ALBERT, ONE HUNDRED TODAY,
ATTRIBUTES HIS FITNESS TO 'X' –
A LIFE-DRUG KNOWN ONLY TO HIM!
(One is reminded of Ferret
in Smollett's *Launcelot Greaves*
'. . . this here Elixir of Long Life,
if properly used, will protract
your days till you shall have seen
your country ruined.')

                                Of course
it will still take us by surprise –
nine out of ten oafs in the street,
a census informs me with cheer,
fondly imagine we'll find
deposits of copper and oil
ad nauseam, or find substitutes.
Possibly; possibly not.
Meanwhile, CIPEC and OPEC
won't *give* it away, we will pay –
or, atavistically, war.

As the Leisure Pages observe,
EARLY RETIREMENT IS COMING.

* *Black Holes*, edited by Cecile De Witt and Bryce S. De Witt (Gordon &
Breach, 1974).

If ever the headlines strike home,
and they see there's nothing to lose,
the nine out of ten will run riot
as these on the Sports Page – terraces
dripping with apes' blood (the same
lovelies, I think, who enriched
the bogs with the following legend
HEADBUTTS AND BOOTS IS OUR BIZNUSS
SHAGGERS IS RULERS OK?) –
yes, add to the cumulate threats,
amassing at x to the nth,
insurrection civil and bloody –
Homo erectus autophagous.

F.T. Index down 1 p.c.
Frankly, we couldn't care less.

Never let it be said that *we*
ever stood in the way of regress.

10 × 10 × 10

One winter evening, Donald travelled the
15 miles to his girl-friend's home town and,
disliking her parents, decided to
phone her house and arrange to rendezvous
at the end of her road rather than call
for her and have to face her mum and dad.
Her mother answered the phone and said that
Susan was visiting a friend next door.
'Where are you ringing from?' 'Oh, I'm at home.'
(He was, in fact, only round the corner.)

Having put down the phone, he decided
to walk to the house next door to Susan's,
collect her from there and go to the pub
(thus still avoiding her parents). He set
off along the road where the kiosk was
and, after a few minutes, turned at right
angles into Susan's road and sauntered
towards her friend's; when all of a sudden
out of the pitch darkness bounded a dog
which he recognized as Sue's Dalmatian.

A distant street light illumined a pair,
identified by Don as Sue's parents
(which identification was confirmed
by her mother's voice shouting 'Heel, Measles!'
– he well knew both voice and nomenclature).
Rightly judging that they might find it odd
to encounter one who had telephoned
only five minutes ago and told them
emphatically that he was 15 miles
distant, he panicked and turned on his heel.

He walked briskly away from them, but thought,
as he passed under a sodium light,
that they might recognize him, so he hunched
his back – hoping thus to disguise his frame.
He lacked confidence in this, however,
and to consolidate his disguise he
affected a limp – first left leg, then right.
Thus, alternating legs, he limped faster
and faster away from her parents, till
he was limp-sprinting at 10 m.p.h.

But Measles, who knew him, tore after him,
yelping and biting his trouser leg. 'Down,
bad Measles!' he whispered between clenched teeth
while oscillating extravagantly.
He paused at the corner, smacked Measles' snout,
said 'Damn and blast it all to bloody Hell!',
ran his fastest (unhampered by Measles
and now using conventional techniques)
and thought 'This could be good to write about
– but in the third person, naturally.'

On another occasion, Donald was
out drinking with a friend when closing time
came, so, wishing to continue their chat,
they went to a theatre which also
had a restaurant serving drinks till 12.
Drinks were only served to people dining
and, not wanting anything to eat, Don
went to the bar for two pints of bitter.
'No drinks without meals, sir.' 'Oh, we've just got
our meal, over on that table.' he lied.

'You're a bloody liar – you've only just
come in. Get out. You're not getting served.' So
he left by one of three doors and went down
a dark corridor. But it must have been
the wrong door, because he found himself in
a huge auditorium – house lights dimmed,
only the stage lights ablaze – completely
deserted. He stumbled along the aisle
to the stage, which he mounted, noticing
a stage *on* the stage – 10 × 10 × 10.

He clambered up to the stage on the stage
and sang Maurice Chevalier numbers,
danced to the empty auditorium.
'Evry leel briz sim to weesper Looiz.
Eef a natingel coo sing lak you. Sank
Even for leetel girls – zey grow up in
ze mos delightfool away. Ooh la la!
Eet is – ow you Eenglish say? – saucy, no?'
Behind him, twenty feet high, he noticed
a catwalk reached by a metal ladder.

He climbed the ladder and danced along the
foot-wide catwalk. 'Evry leel briz sim to' –
suddenly he lost balance and fell but
clutched at the back-drapes to save himself and
thought 'I am an interloper, therefore
I must do nothing to damage this hall.'
Thinking his weight would rip the curtains, he
let go, fell down a few feet, grabbed hold, then
let go again and grabbed hold again till
the fabric began to tear and conscience

forced Don to let go for fear of damage.
*   *   *   *   *   *   *   *   *   *
*   *   *   *   *   *   *   *   *   *
*   *   *   *   *   *   When he regained
consciousness, he was considering the
arbitrary nature of the Sonnet –
'One might as well invent any kind of
structure (ten stanzas each of ten lines each
of ten syllables might be a good one),
the subject matter could be anything.'

Receipt (1793)

For Cancer – boil some finest Turkey figs
in newest milk, applying them as hot
as can be scarcely borne onto the Cancer
which must be washed 11 times a day
in the milk (warmed). The figs must be applied
fresh in the morning, once or twice by day
and in the night. The quantity of figs
to be boiled up each time, to be proportioned
unto the size of that place to be covered.
The use of this cure must be persevered in
for 3 or 4 months. An old man was cured
of most inveterate Cancer (which began
festering at one corner of his mouth,
had eat clean thro' his cheek and half way down
his throat) with only six pounds of best figs.
A woman was, in the like manner, cured,
being afflicted ten years with a Cancer.
Her breast was used to bleed so exceedingly
that it was by the Faculty supposed
to be an ulcer. By repeating figs
three times, it stopped – employing only 12
pounds of best Turkey figs. First application
of the said poultice is attended with
a deal of pain, but after that the patient
finds ease and much relief with every fresh one.
To cure the Cancer if inveterate,
eat only turnips boiled and turnips' liquor.
At these times, you don't drink the milk, nor have
no beer, wine or spirits, which inflames
the blood that by the Cancer is inflamed –
a person was of Rheumatism cured,
another of the Scurvey in two months
with this most efficacious mode of living
and air and exercise which cleared the blood
of all unclean inflammatory heat.
For Hectic Fever and for Spitting Blood,

Consumption on the lungs et cetera –
bleeding is serviceable, and a diet
of Whorehound Plantain mixed in Buttermilk
in the fresh vapours of some country town.
A person was by this receipt quite cured
of Heart Affliction, sometimes called Love Gout.

From FICTION

(Verse is <u>not</u> Fiction –
ask any librarian)

Fiction

Donald is a fictitious character
arrived at an age and bodily state
rendering suicide superfluous,
would rather sip Grands Crus than throw his leg.
He is a writer of fiction. He says
'Even one's self is wholly fictitious'.
Hatred once drew him to satiric verse
but he could think of nothing to rhyme with
'Manageress of the Angel Hotel',
or 'I call my doctor "*Killer*" *Coldwill*'
(a fictitious name, 'Coldwill', by the way),
or 'Headmaster of the Secondary Mod.'

Donald has created a character
called 'Donald' or 'Don' who keeps a notebook
dubbed 'Donald's Spleneticisms', e.g.:
'Complacent as a Country Town G.P.',
'Contemptible as County Council Clerks',
'A hateful little Welshman shared my train
with no lobes to his ears and yellow socks',
'Seedy as Salesmen of Secondhand Cars'.

In Donald's novel, 'Don' writes poetry –
titles such as 'It's a Small World', 'Fiction',
'Y – X', 'Remaindered', which he sends
to literary periodicals
under the nom de plume '*Peter Reading*'
(the present writer is seeking advice
from his attorney, Donald & Donald).
This fictitious bard has a doctor called
'Coldwill' who sleeps with the manageress
of the Angel (and sues 'Don' for libel).

In Donald's novel, 'Don' (whose nom de plume
is *Peter Reading*') sues a man whose *real*
name is 'Peter Reading' for having once
written a fiction about a poet
who wrote verse concerning a novelist
called 'Donald' whose book 'Fiction' deals with 'Don'
(a poet who writes satirical verse
and is sued by an incompetent quack,
the manageress of a pub, a Celt
with lobeless ears and yellow socks, acned
Council clerks and a Range Rover salesman).

In 'Reading's' fiction, the poet who writes
verse concerning the novelist 'Donald'
is sued by the latter who takes offence
at the lines '. . . an age and bodily state
rendering suicide superfluous,
would rather sip Grands Crus than throw his leg'.
For the Defence, 'Donald, Q.C.' says that
'Even one's self is wholly fictitious'.

Y – X

X daily drove the 7.15 from Stretton.
Y, whom he shared the task with, remarks this:
'Six foot, ee were, ex-pug. Sometimes eed *stare* . . .
– but mostly, like, ee seemed like any other
bloke (but they always do) – eed put a bet on
and, Satdy nights, used to get on the piss.
Lived, since I knowed im, with is crippled mother.
– Angd isself dressed in ladies' underwear.'

5

Livid green fingers
quarter a two-inch
disc (3 a.m.). Dark.
Grid of window-frame
on the wall throbs blue.

. . . tickticktickticktick-
tickticktickticktick . . .
Klaxon: eee-ow, *eee-
ow*, eee-ow, *eee-ow*
EEE-OW, *EEE-OW*. Brake

Aromatic mint.
When inhalation
suddenly ceases,
a yearn for scent of
household-dust even.

Peppermint tablet
reduces to chalk.
Though bitter, each grain
at the last moment
is sweet to the tongue.

Fretfully twisted
grip of moist bed-sheet
in senile fist helps
relieve a weight like
wet sand-bag on chest.

Kingfisher-blue light
each second. White door.
Scarlet cross. Black flask
labelled 0$_2$. Black
peaked cap. One-way glass.

. . . RESPIRATORY
WILCO. HASTENING
(BLEEP; BLEEP) CASUALTY
ALL SPEED. MESSAGE TIMED
O THREE SEVENTEEN . . .

Vying with Dettol,
nicotine wafts from
ambulance-man's hands
each side my bald head.
Rubber oxygen.

Sometimes demotic
is also precise
viz: mouth now tastes like
the bottom of a
budgerigar's cage.

As if tight thonging
bound the diaphragm.
Itchy coarse blanket.
The palm sweaty of
someone's hand held tight.

Sir, in flannel bags,
beckoning boys in.
Eyes, blurred with speed, note
Higgo's black toe-cap
stuck out. Ground rises.

Roar: TWO-FOUR-SIX- EIGHT,
WHO-DO-WE-AP-REE-
CI-ATE? C-O-L-
L-E-G-I-A-
T-E, COLLEGIATE ! ! !

Spearmint. First mowings
off the Games Field. School-
Meals-Service-van-stink.
Earth, pungent sphagnum.
Metallic blood reek.

Beech Nut chewy. Then
grate of sour grit/sweet
shoots of spring grass. Then
nasal blood swallowed,
cupric – of pence sucked.

Stitch under ribs aches.
Sucked air sore on lungs.
Ground battering soles.
Knees, muzzle, chest, palms,
smashed concurrently.

Close-up of boob in
flotsam of torn-off
tights, pants; beyond which
3 a.m. shows on
the travelling-clock.

Purr of a zip. Moan.
Rustle. A hiss of
silk stroked. A gasp. Quick
deep inhalation.
Regular squelch. Quiet.

Sabaean parfum
des arbres singuliers,
verts tamariniers,
des fruits savoureux.
Cheesy pudenda.

Colgate with fluoride.
Slurping tongues, after
an hour, remind one
of well-hung partridge
(followed by Roquefort).

Opulent soft flesh
cool on belly and
thighs concurrently.
Painful release/bliss —
a bit like a sneeze.

Polished steel basin
containing lancets
mirrors crow's-feet. Cup
clamped on nose and mouth.
Ensoresque mask leers.

Steel trolley clatters.
Gush, as of Ocean
heard in a shell, falls;
rises; falls; rises;
falls. A voice gasps 'Christ!'

Meths, Dettol, laundered
linen, TCP,
PVC, rubber.
Sinus contracts to
vinegar, copper.

Viscid foul spit. Plaque
licked from my own tongue
tastes of overhung
game or Bombay Duck.
Suddenly cupric.

Throb of a tube in
larynx and gullet.
Pressure of tight mask
pinching the muzzle.
Sheet scrapes over pate.

You Can't Be Too Careful

Reports, unfortunately, indicate
Warble infections reaching record peaks.

Statistics from the 1974
National Survey show 40%
Fluke infestation of the British Isles.

Nematodirus could be with us SOON! –
our drench eliminates this deadly worm!

Fluke may have been ingested since September:
this can be countered using Flukanide.

Beware of ORF! Eliminate Grass Staggers!
By treating NOW eradicate those Warbles!

Where Swayback has occurred before, inject
(do not give orally) in pregnancy.

Spray NOW with Cobalt Sulphate – prevent Pine!

Where Worm Burden is evident, e.g.
Scouring or marked Unthriftiness etc.,
drench physically or use granules or dust.

Treat Bowel & Stomach Worm with Bovicam!

It is COMPULSORY to dip for SCAB!
Control Scab AND Mycotic Dermatitis!

Use added CHLORFENVINPHOS to protect
against Fly Strike (also Lice, Keds and Ticks).

No danger of abortion with THIS liquid!

Spray this solution freely on all parts –
especially legs, face and genitals.

Don't let Lungworm Husk catch *you* unawares!

Inter-City

He reads 'But the most unusual thing
about him is his teeth. They are dentures
but they are not ivory. They're made of
some sort of metal, some say steel, others
Duralumin. Anyway, they give him
a somewhat sinister appearance when
he shows them, as he does when he smiles.' He
replaces the book* in his slimline brief-
case and produces *Pun & Ink* (*The Life
of Thomas Hood*) which he pretends to read.

A newly-arrived fellow-passenger
attempts the *Guardian* crossword for five
minutes then says 'Excuse me, put I can't
help noticing se pook you're reating. You
atmire sat piographer, to you?' A
monocle magnifies one cobalt eye.
'I *am* that biographer' lies Donald.
'I take it you've heard of me?' 'Heart of you!
I haf stutiet you altogeser! Please,
I am Liebgarten, Doctor Liebgarten.'

Patent heels click. 'Particularly I
atmire your ferse translation of Kokur
Niznegorsky's heroic anthem *The
Soya Bean Canning-Plant Operative*,
vitch, I unterstant, you hat to smuggle
out of its country of origin in
your untervear. *Nornu of Fitful-head
– Her Influence on Ted Hughes's Later
Style* also I like. Tell me, vot are you
going to write apout in se next von?'

---

* *Biggles Takes a Holiday* by Captain W.E. Johns (Hodder & Stoughton, 1949).

'I have in mind the story of a chap
who went to work in the kitchens of a
celebrated West End hotel – washing
dishes, cooking breakfasts, cleaning ovens,
scrubbing floors, assisting the Assistant
Chef and suchlike quite disagreeable
activities. Having for some months held
this respectable position, he fell
into the habitual practice of
filching his Sunday supper from the fridge.

This hebdomadary beano was quite
contrary to the expectations of
the establishment – which, whilst providing
nourishment for employees, neglected
the sophisticated requirements of
our hero. He purchased, from Berry Bros.
& Rudd, a case of halves of Clos de Bèze
1961 to accompany
the cold roast partridge purloined each Sabbath.
Soon the game was up. The management guessed.

A padlock was put on the coldstore door
and he was summoned to the manager's
office. "Now then, Donald," the manager
said "to be perfectly honest with you,
over the last few weeks a number of
items have gone missing out of the fridge.
What do you think of that?" "I am shocked, sir,
deeply deeply shocked." "So are we. That's why
we've decided to entrust you alone
of all our under-staff with the fridge key."

Until the first day of February
(the end of the partridge shooting season)
no Sunday passed without *Perdix perdix*
enhancing our hero's willow-pattern.'
'Pravo! Unt I am remintet now of
a man like your Tonalt who vent to vork
se kitchen of a restaurant in Soho.
First in se morning his jop vas to mop
se floors – who vas alvays covert in grease
especially rount se foot of se stove.

Vell, in se kitchen corner vas kept a
fire extinguisher on se floor, unt von
morning vile mopping he picket it up
to mop petter in se corner. Vell, he
replact se fire extinguisher ven he
hat moppt put it vas a preak-pottle type
unt se force of his putting it town must
have proken se pottle – Achtung! he cries
unt foam is schpurting everyvere unt he
picks up se frightful sing in alarm unt

turns arount looking for somevere to schvirt
it harmlessly. Alas! on se stove is
a four foot long salmon poaching gently.
Vooosh! it is coatet in five inch of fizz.
Schpinning rount in fright, still holting se fire
extinguisher, he fizzes se Het Chef.
Soon he is packing his pags unt leaving.'
Laughter, then five minutes silence follows.
'Soon you are reaching your testination!
You see how kvickiy your journey passes!

Now you vill sign your latest pook for me!'
Hands him a sumptuous work entitled
Dis Quiet, or The Devil's Kitchen in
full polished tree calf, gilt in compartments,
crimson lettering-pieces, dentelles, all
edges uncut, all pages blank, only
the water-mark GARDEN CITY. Train stops.
'Where the Hell is this? Who the Hell are you?'
'I am Liebgarten, Doctor Liebgarten.'
The Doctor smiles, showing his metal teeth.

Parallel Texts

(A bucolic employee of
South Shropshire Farmers Ltd)

You remembers that old boy Marsh?
    – im as lived at Stokesay?
     – forever pickin is nose?
   Well, this mornin ees takin
     some cattle over the line
(course they got underpass, like,
    but also the level crossin
      as mostly they uses),
      an 7.15 from Stretton
       runs over the fucker
 – course kills im, like, never
you seen such a mess, cows an all.
    Still, it dunna matter a lot
     – ee were daft as a coot.

(The Craven Arms, Stretton
& Tenbury Advertiser)

A Stokesay farmer was killed
when he was struck by a train
on a stretch of track near
Craven Arms. He was Mr John
Jeremiah Marsh, a 60-year-old
bachelor of Stokesay Castle
Farm, and the accident occurred
just yards from his home, at
Stokeswood – an unmanned level
crossing. Mr Marsh is thought
to have been opening the gate.
The train which struck him
was pulling 39 goods wagons
on its way to Carlisle.

Mens Talents in Difcours Shadowed out by Muficall Inftruments *

Your Drums are blufterers in difcours, that with a loudnefs domineer in publick over men of better fenfe and fill the place with a rattling found: yt hath feldom any wit in it: it's the emptinefs yt makes it found.

The Lute is directly oppofite to the Drum and founds very fweet and low: the Lutonifts are therefore men of a fine genius, great affability and efteemed chiefly by men of good tafte.

The Trumpet hath but 4 or 5 nots and points out to us men that have learned a fmoothnefs of difcours from the polite company they have kept but have fhallow parts and weak judgements: a play houfe, a drawing room, a ball, a vifiting day, are the few nots they are mafters of.

Violins are your lively forward wits that diftinguifh themfelves by yt fharpnefs of their flourifhes.

Your Bafs Viols yt rumbles in ye bottom of the Confort may fignifie men of rough gener who do not love to hear themfelves talk but fometimes break out into an agreeable bluntnefs in company.

As for country wits yt talk with great elagunce: of hares: horfes: quickfet hedges: 5 bard gates: double ditches and broken hocks: muft take up with the tittle of an Hunting Horn.

The Bagpipes yt entertains you from morning till night with a repetition of the fame nots are ye dull heavy fellows: ftory tellers that with a perpetuall humming quite tire your patience.

* Adapted from *D. Donaldfonne His Booke Anno Dom 1713* in the author's poffeffion.

80

Harpficords yt are a kind of Confort by themfelves are perfons who re mafters of every kind of converfation and can talk of all fubjects: f which kind there are but few.

Your men that talk of nothing but what is melancholly and look upon mirth as criminall fhall be tirmed Paffing Bells.

The mufick of the Flute is the converfation of a mild amiable woman t fooths the ear and fills it with a gentle kind of melody as keeps the mind awake without ftartling it: as raifes an agreeable paffion between tranfport and indolence.

The Hautboy is the moft perfect of the Flute fpecies which with all he fweetnefs of found hath a great ftrength and variety of nots. The Hautboy in this fex is as fcarce as the Harpficord in ye other.

That woman who fancys herfelf a wit and difpifes the mufick of the Flute as low and infipit and ftrives to entertain with tart obfervations pert fancies and little turns muft be a Flageolet. The Flageolets among their own fex are more efteemed than the Flutes.

The woman that diftinguifhes herfelf by a great many fkittifh nots: affected fqueaks and is more jiggifh than the Fiddle itfelf muft be called a Kitt.

The women with grave cenfures of vice: fupercilious cafts of ye eye and a feeming contempt for lightnefs of converfation diftinguifh hemfelves for to be known by the name of that ancient ferious matron-like inftrument the Virginal.

Your young country lady who with a great deal of mirth and nnocence diverts the company very agreeably: by the wildnefs of her nots I would have fignified a Lancafhire Hornpipe: your ramps and bording fchool girls fall under this denomination.

A Welch Harp is an inftrument which very much delights in th
tunes of ould hiftoricall ballads: by this I would therefore defcribe
lady that talks of pedigrees and defcents and finds herfelf related t
almoft every great family in England for which caufe fhe jarrs and i
often out of tune in company for want of their due attention to her

She that accompanys her difcours with motions of ye body: toffes c
the head: brandifhes of the fan: whofe mufick is loud and mafculin
and fets fomeone or other blufhing fhall be a Kettle Drum.

Your larum houfehould fcaulds or impertinent tittle tattles wh
have no other variety in difcours but that of talking flower or fafte
are to be Caftinets or Jews Harps: all tongue.

Confidering how abfolutely neceffary it is that two inftrument
which are to play together for life fhould be exactly tund and go i
perfect confort with each other: I would propofe matches betweer
the mufick of both fexts according to the following table of
marriage

Drum & Kettle Drum
Lute & Flute
Harpficord & Hautboy
Violin & Flageolet
Bafs Viol & Kitt
Trumpet & Welch Harp
Hunting Horn & Hornpipe
Bagpipe & Caftinet
Paffing Bell & Virginal.

In State *

Wedged matchsticks, Visitor,
lurk at the back of
the serene smile.

Set in crystal,
the waxy finger
can touch no trigger,
nor the opulent slipper
trample to be kissed.

Behind: ranks of cut blooms,
and little birds tethered
by tiny golden links.

*

From the Spanish of Pedro Ximénez's *Sobre la muerte del generalísimo el
xcelentísimo Sr. conde de Torregamberro.*

Mystery Story

One day, the scarcely-known poet received the following:

'Baudelaire'
Mill Street
Huddersfield

Dear Mr R * * * * * g,

      I hope you won't mind me writing to you in this way but I felt I had to, having just read your latest volume of verse recently published by Secker & Warburg, who were kind enough to supply me with your address. Your work was first drawn to my attention by a review in the Times Literary Supplement by Gavin Ewart. I was so impressed by this that I bought a copy next day and read it in one sitting. What can I say? W.H. Auden (the later works of course), Roy Fuller, Philip Larkin, Dylan Thomas, George MacBeth – truly you belong to our magnificent heritage of Great Bards! I have tried without success to get hold of your other books. Are they out of print, perhaps?

      It may be of interest to you to know that I am the Secretary of our local Poetry Club – a very modest group, I can assure you, of amateur poets and versifiers who get together once a fortnight on a Thursday to read to one another and compare notes. Recently we have invited a number of well-known writers to speak to us about their work and to read extracts. So far this year we have listened to Roger Parbett, Edward Lucie-Smith and the novelist Rachael Summers. Next year, I hope, we shall have Jon Silkin and Percy Nicholson. Would you, I wonder, be interested in joining us sometime? We do, of course, pay a modest fee (generally in the region of £10) plus all expenses. Usually the guest speaker is accommodated for the night at the home of one of our members, and my wife and I would be only too happy to put you up should you decide to come – pure selfishness on our part, I can assure you!

      Once again may I express my great admiration for your work and say that I look forward to hearing from you in

the near future. I enclose a stamped addressed envelope.
                    Yours very sincerely,
                        Alfred E.Hound.

Simultaneously covering the likelihood of the letter being from a
duper and the unlikely contingency of its being the work of a bona
fide lunatic, the scarcely-known poet replied:

Dear Mr Hound,
            I am entrusted, during the absence of Mr R * * * * * g,
with answering his correspondence.
            I feel certain he will be gratified to read your adulatory
opinion of his latest volume and am happy to be able to advise
you that, as far as I am aware, his previous collections are still
in print and, no doubt, available through any reputable book-
seller.
            I cannot say whether Mr R * * * * * g will be in a
position to take up your kind offer of speaking to your local
poetry organization, but upon his return I shall naturally direct
his attention to your letter, when he will doubtless be delight-
ed to contact you if he is able to accept.
            Once again, I wish to express the deepest gratitude
on behalf of Mr R * * * * * g for your favourable and encourag-
ing letter.
                    Yours faithfully,
                        Donald Donaldson
                    (per procurationem P * * * r R * * * * * g).

Some weeks later, the scarcely-known poet received the following:

Dear Mr R * * * * * g,
            Forgive me writing to you again and taking up more
of your valuable time, but as I have not heard from you following
my earlier letter, I wondered if I might presume even further
by suggesting a little meeting. At least this would avoid your
having to employ your pen on such mundane matters when it
could be used to such good effect elsewhere!
            It so happens that my wife and I will be visiting some
relatives in Llandrindod Wells next weekend and, as we will

be passing close by your town, I wondered if we might call on you with a view to discussing your possible visit to our poetry group in Huddersfield. Even if you cannot find the time to make the journey north, both my wife and I would greatly enjoy the chance to meet you in the flesh, having had up to now only a rather tendentious view of you through your excellent verse. We should hope to call around mid-day on Saturday, so perhaps we could have a drink with our little chat – I know what poets are!

By the bye, although I am not familiar with your town, I believe it was once the home of the well-known folk-bard and farmer Fred Jordan. Perhaps you know him?

I hope this arrangement meets with your approval as we are both 'dying' to meet you. We look forward to your reply. Perhaps you would be good enough to enclose street directions or, even better, a map.

Yours sincerely,

Alfred E. Hound.

The scarcely-known poet (abstractedly addressing his reply to 'Rimbaud', Mill Street, Huddersfield) answered:

Dear Mr Hound,

Thank you for your recent letter – that which you sent me previously was, I understand, dealt with by Mr Donaldson on my behalf.

I am fascinated to learn that you have relatives in the Welsh place you mention and that your visiting them there will occasion your arrival here at mid-day on Saturday next.

Since it is my custom to eat lunch at the time you mention, I trust you will not find it unamusing to share my mahogany and claret bottle on that day.

I am not acquainted with the bucolic gentleman, Fred Jervis or Jardine, whom you are anxious to trace.

I possess no maps.

Yrs. &c.

P * * * R * * * * * g.

Some days later, this last letter was RETURNED TO SENDER in a POST OFFICE RETURNED POSTAL PACKET No. 449 as UNDELIVERED FOR REASON STATED – ADDRESS NOT KNOWN. No more was heard of Hound.

That was thirty years ago. The career of the scarcely-known poet is nearly over. Sometimes, in the early hours of the morning, he lies, confronting obscurity, pondering the true identity of Alfred E. Hound.

Opinions of the Press

I am an abrasive wit,
an oasis of intellect.

Of my kind –
and there are not many of my kind – ·
I am really quite remarkably good.

I am mordant, very mordant.
Satire is clearly one of my gifts.

Out of everyday matters
I fashion urbane jokes.

My evocation of a seedy hotel room
is particularly liked.

Most of me is marked
by a bitter sense of humour.

I am reminiscent of
intellectual paper-games.

I can handle the Long Poem.

I contain some clever rhymes –
e.g. candid/Gran did.

I am a master of the narrative.
I am a master of the descriptive.

I am looked forward to
being heard from in the future.

ON THE OTHER HAND

I do not transcend pain with Poetry.

I am not as mellifluous as Sir John Betjeman.

I am not as good as
a very great number of people
(who do the same thing better).

Not all of me makes you laugh aloud
on the number 17 bus.

I am drab rhythmless demotic.

I am all very amusing in my way, maybe,
(and definitely mordant)
but am I Art?

From TOM O'BEDLAM'S BEAUTIES

(I once considered nursing them
— even went for an interview
— magnanimous of me, eh?

Backed out — like them, eschewing
the risky Real for Illusion.)

?

Sired by *Surgical   Sundries Inc.*,
my appearance – patent   pending – is awesome.
I am not fettled from   fleeces of thick wool,
no knitter's needles   knocked me up.
Silkworms that dextrously   adorn the sleek web
with *wyrda cræftum*   couldn't make me;
yet, in institutions,   internationally
men will attest me   a tight-fitting raiment.

Say, supple-minded   master of wit,
wealthy in words,   what my name is.

Alma Mater

A rather solitary boy –
we were hardly aware of him until
one day, when we were in 5C,
in Assembly, as the Assistant Head
was intoning the Lord's Prayer, he sang

> If you go down to the woods today
> You'd better not go alone,
> It's lovely down in the woods today
> But safer to stay at home

loud and was removed during the second verse.

About a week later, in Chemistry,
Mr Watts discovered him writing up
his account of the preparation of
sodium thiosulphate crystals
in an unusual manner i.e.
he would do a few lines and then invert
his exercise book before scrawling
the next bit – alternate paragraphs
upside-down. When asked why, he replied
'In Japan the natives eat fish raw.'

Some days later, he seized Mr Hotchkiss
(a small History teacher) by the throat
crying 'At the roadside rooks snatch voles!'.

About three-quarters of the way through
the Autumn Term, he left (I believe
to conclude his education elsewhere).

Hardfhip Aboard American Sloop The Peggy, 1765

Sailed for New York from Azores,
October 24th,
American floop the *Peggy*
(Mafter, Captain Harrifon),
cargo of wine and brandy
alfo a negro flave.

Storm blew up from North-Eaft,
rigging feverely damaged,
could make no way, d'ye fee?
Harrifon rationed all hands,
one pound of dry bread per day,
one pint of water and wine.

Hull fprung breach below water,
two veffels paffed – foul conditions
prevented communications,
rations reduced by degrees,
no food or water remained,
hands drunk on brandy and wine.

By December 25th
clement weather prevailed,
a fail was fpied, but its fkipper,
damn his eyes, ignored our fignal,
all hands pierced the air with fcreams
more pitiful than mews' wails.

Only liveftock aboard –
two pigeons and the fhip's cat,
doves flain for Chriftmas Dinner,
flew the cat two days later,
divided it into nine,
head was the Captain's portion.

After the cat, the negro.
Fell on his knees, begged mercy.
Dragged him into the fteerage,
fhot through the head by James Doud.
Kindled a fire abaft
to fry entrails and liver.

Mr James Campbell, half ftarved,
rufhed forward, ripped out the liver,
ftuffed it raw into his mouth.
The reft of us, after feafting,
pickled the body's remains –
threw head and fingers o'erboard.

James Campbell died raving mad
three days later, from eating
the liver raw. Fearing much,
left we all contract his madnefs,
refrained from eating Campbell,
caft body unto the fea.

By January 26th
the corpfe of the flave was ate.
Drew lots to fee who was next,
myfelf, David Flat, foremaft man,
felected the fhorteft ftraw,
afked to be defpatched quickly.

Reft of the hands decided
to wait till 11 o'clock
next day before flaying me
left deliverance fhould arrive.
That night my fenfes quit me –
'tis faid they have not returned.

At 10 a veffel hove-to,
the *Sufannah* bound for London
(Mafter, Thomas Evers),
took furvivors aboard,
myfelf in a fwoon, raving,
reached Land's End March 2nd.

To this day fometimes I fee them:
Captain David Harrifon,
James Doud, Lemuel Afhley,
James Warren, Samuel Wentworth,
eyes like a frightened horfe's
of the neger, whites uplifted.

Tom o' Bedlam's Beauties*

In the summer hols we cycled
as far as the green water-tower
in the grounds of which grew apples.

Broken Bass bottles, embedded
in the cement-skimmed wall,
we bridged with tough hide school satchels.

Once within, we filched unripe
fruit – English old-fashioned names
like *Tom o' Bedlam's Beauties*.

The water-tower watchman, too,
had old-fashioned lingo – 'Grrr!
Young varmints!' – as in the *Beano*.

Returning, we munched apples under
another red brick buttressed wall.
Sated, we sought diversion.

Scaling a steep brick triangle,
peering over the parapet,
a prison-like scene was presented.

Close-cropped men in brown denim
tended a formal flower garden
behind which, a house with barred windows.

The nearest gardener glopped
but seemed not to see us, holding
his rake upside-down by the prongs.

*Old Herefordshire name for variety of eating-apple.

Another solemnly knelt
chewing the bloom of a red
Hybrid Tea – *Ena Harkness*, I think.

We pelted them with our cores
and all we could not consume.
Some of us scored direct hits.

The one with the upside-down rake
raised his palms to the sky
and visibly, audibly, wept.

Gigglingly biking back,
we resolved to repeat the prank
discreetly dubbed *Sanes and Loonies.*

Bereft

The only one left who could use a scythe
in all Onibury, or pleach a hedge
the *old* way: but could not understand
how the electric cooker worked or
(and this takes some believing) the light switched on –
when his wife died he sat in the dark, hungry.

Dialled the Surgery with my assistance,
held the phone in two paws like a sad dog
gnawing a bone, not knowing which end spoke.

Wandering

Permit me to parley – Brigadier Peregrine
Fashpoint-Shellingem (author of *Peruvian
Jungle by Kayak, With a Kodak in Kooju,
Huskies Away! Hottentots Were My Neighbours,
In the Bush with the Blacks of Booloo-Kishooloo,*
&c. &c. &c. &c.),
K.C.B., M.V.O., F.R.G.S.

        Oh, I
know that I probably don't seem the type, as we
prune back this gnarled Hybrid Tea *Ena Harkness* and
rake the first leaves from the lawns to the compost heaps
tucked in triangular shadows of buttresses
(daily, the sun getting lower, the wall higher),
but, I assure you, the world *was* my whatsaname
(damn funny thing; can't remember the word for it).

Camped with the Indians, pure Tehuelche blood,
on the bleak plateaux of cold Patagonia,
cattle crashed down under bowled bolladores there –
feet drawn together noosed, tail stuck up rigidly.

Saw summers on the Salween when the river rose
fifty feet overnight flinging up cottage-sized
boulders like pitched pebbles, porters splashed into pulp.

Camped at the edge of the East Rongbuk Glacier,
gale reached its maximum, 1 a.m. 26th,
wild flapping canvas made noise like machine-gun fire,
fine frozen spindrift thrashed into our sleeping-bags.
Jettisoning empty oxygen-cylinders,
each clanged like church-bell rings into the East Rongbuk.

Fell through the floes with a dog-team in Labrador,
slashed free the harnesses, swam for the nearest ice,
stripped off my garments and beat the freeze out of 'em,
still couldn't last the night, had to kill all the dogs,
skinned 'em and made a rough coat with the hair inside, .
piled up the dead bodies, cuddled up close to 'em,
lasted till morning, relief-ship arrived, by Gad.

Plied down the Pyrene River in wild Peru,
Indian, Quinchori, built twenty rafts for us,
bartered with five rolls of cloth, knives and ornaments,
balsa logs pinned with hard splinters of chonta wood,
spray flew on all sides up, rainbowing rays of sun . . .

Sometimes it seems a long, long while ago to me . . .
all I can do to remember events when that
damnation Matron, whatever her name is, says
'Now then, of *course* you're a brave, brave explorer man.
Tell Doctor' (whatsisname) 'Snyderson all about
nice Patagonia, *"Brigadier"* Peregrine.'

Artemus' Wardrobe

Gents Owtfitters, now, hold me in grate or,
becuz the following befell me wunce.

Requiring britches and a dressing-gown,
I haysund to the neyburhood Booteek
and did not find it difficult to chuze
garments appropriate to my fizzeek.
The Chaingin Room wuz fitted with a daw
sitch as Salunes have in a Wild West town –
opening both ways, maid of slats of wood,
exposing heds an neez but not full-frunce.
I dond the Paisley robe with greater plum
and vood the mirrer with a grate enthoos.
But, hitchin up the trowzerz, as I stood
balansin on wun legg, I nearly cumm
a cropper – hopt ter save meself, an lent
on the accursid daw. It throo me owt.
I hopt a pays ore too, wylst givin vent
too me emowshunz, & herd someone showt
'A Bedlamite, got luce without is droors!' –
the most embarrassust I ever bean.
The ground flew up and hit me on all fores.
I girdid up my Lions & fled the Seen.

Some of Their Efforts*

How unnerving to meet Dr Schynieder
& his burly white-coated apprentice
with his Jungian remarks
& a skull-cap that sparks
& a stiff reinforced canvas jacket
& a plaque ready-labelled HIC+IACET
PEREGRINVS+NON+COMPOS+MENTIS.

How diverting to see one's companions
involuntarily flex their thighs
as their wires are plugged in
with a matronly grin
by Nurse who manipulates wails
as a virtuoso scales
in a two finger exercise.

* See Glibber & Crass, 'Therapeutic value of Poetry practised amongst the mentally disturbed,' Feb. 1979, 'Transact. Soc. Cephalic Research,' p. 119. For the strong tendency in our nearest allies, the monkeys, in microcephalous idiots, and in the barbarous races of mankind, to imitate whatever they hear, see Vogt, *'Mémoire sur les Microcéphales,'* 1867, p. 169.

Natives are nice, they call me 'Bwana',
only their lingo is loco – they call
the Belgian Congo 'Ward 17B'.
Last night I fought a croc underwater;
Medicine-Man said it was a 'Mattress'.
In this jungle coons wear white linen coats.
Shhh! There ventures the wily okapi.
I have perfected swinging on creepers,
slow-motion grandfather-clock pendulum
over the canyon bosky with palm fronds,
creamy the foaming creek, the water-hole
harbouring hippopotami. Pygmies
are awe-struck at my *Aaoo-aaoo-aas*!
Chimps are my chums. Jane wears cheetah-skin bras.

Extruding absentmindedly remorse
incalculable providential croon
reflect resourceful Japanese fish course
interminable efflorescent spoon;
landed excruciating gentry meant
intestinal unease – th' Olympic Champ.
Wherefore go jovial unto thy tent
wherein, betimes, walls wax exceeding damp.

Nevertheless, Concord with Hybrid Tea
conspires withal, crass Patagonian
Sales Managers are here and so are we.
Up, Jenkins, heretofore Etonian,
grid up your lioness, escaler wall!
Thrall! Thrall, rapscallion! Thrall! Thrall! Thrall! Thrall!

Phrenfy

The Mafter's phrenfy having continued long,
his left eye fwelled unto an hen's egg fize
fo that the furgeon daily feared 'twould burft.

Th' extreme pain of this tumour caufed the Mafter
to be awake a month. On fome occafion
it took four other perfons and myfelf
to hold him in reftraint 'gainft his defire
to tear his own eye out with his own hands.

Thence he continued filent one whole year.
In this ftate of poor helplefs idiocy
he languifhed.

On November 30th
I went into his chamber – 'twas his birthday,
and bonfires and illuminations marked
th' refpect the townffolk felt at the event.
I fpoke to him about thefe preparations
to which he faid 'All folly, Mrs Ridgeway.
They had done better letting it alone.'

A few months afterwards, on my removing
a fharp knife from his grafp, he faid 'I am
that which I am, I am that which I am'
and in fix minutes, poor fad fimpleton,
whifpered the fame thing two or three times more.

One day, calling his fervant to his fide
but being quite unable to exprefs
any defires, he fhewed figns of diftrefs
and great uneafinefs and faid at length
'I am a fool'. On fome occafion later,
his fervant having taken away his watch,
he called the menial and faid 'Bring it here'.

His laft words, fpoken to his fervant when
that gentleman was breaking a large hard coal,
were, 'That is a ftone, you blockhead'. He was quiet
a twelvemonth afterwards and died in filence.

once inherited a parcel of port from the cellar of an old friend.

walked the two miles from the station to his house in silver February sunshine. The gravel of the long driveway crackled underfoot.

had arranged with National Wine Carriers Ltd. that the cases, a dozen or so, should be collected that day, and, after briefly exchanging greetings with my old army pal's widow, Ethel Fashpoint-Shellingem, I hastened to the cellar, where, by the light of a candle, I applied myself to the pleasurable task of gently removing the old bottles from their bins and crating them in straw for their journey to my own cellars.

When the last of the cases was carefully nailed shut, I proceeded to transfer them one by one up the hollowed stone steps into the hallway to await the arrival of the van.

As I was crossing the thickly carpeted reception room with the last case (a dozen of Noval 'Nacional' '63 – a sort of 'modern pre-phylloxera' from ungrafted vines, truly magnificent wine, still waiting its prime in my bins now, toughness softening, fruit beginning to show beautifully as the spirit integrates . . .), an odd noise from the top of the broad oak staircase caused me to pause.

A noise such as one might use to instruct a horse to accelerate, only higher in pitch – 'Gerrupp-upp-upp' – wafted down from the master bedroom followed by uncontrolled hysterical sobbing followed by 'I simply, gerrupp-upp-upp, can't go on-nn, ho-ho-o-o, God hel-l-p me-e-e'.

hurriedly added the case of 'Nacional' to the others, then evasively slipped out of the front door and down the gravel.

Peregrine's popping off like that must have upset the old bird, I suppose.' I supposed to myself. 'Still, better pull yourself together, Ethel old girl, or you'll end up like poor Perry – finish your days in the Bin.'

At the main gate I met the little chap in the NWC van.

'I say,' I said, 'go easy with those cases o'man – somewhere in tha lot there's a dozen of '27 Taylors (absolutely superb balance and wonderfully long finish, you know) and half a dozen 1857s of ar unknown shipper (probably starting to fade a bit now in fruit and sweetness, becoming rather dry and spirituous, and the colour pale amber by now, I shouldn't be at all surprised).'

Commitment

'Tom's in a "Rest Home" under Doctor Snyde.
Gerald's *so* nice, a carpet-slipper rep., –
he fell head-over-heels for me – I pride
myself on my appearance (it's a step
up in the world to ride round in a Merc.).
About the time of my *affaire* with Gerry,
Tom went right off the rails, ("Pressure of Work"
the Doctor said; he certainly went very
odd – once, when he came home from the office,
he smashed the phone up, shouting "ring-a-ding"
and "burr-burr-burr", then sat, drinking black coffees,
all night). Pressure of Work's a funny thing.
His raving yells, his sobbing and his quarrels
obliged us to commit him to "The Laurels".'

?

Can you guess me? A garment; not knitted, though, nor ornate,
not slinky skin-tight silk nor stretched-transparent tulle,
neither the pelt of the whale nor white North Pole bear.
Royal violet velvet, poxed office-clerks' poplin;
composed of neither of these am I. Classless;
vassal, my stiff canvas fits tight, or viscount.

Without my weave, un-wise would wave their arms weirdly.

From DIPLOPIC

Optician, I am having Double Visions
to see one thing from two sides. Only
give me a Spectacle and I am delighted.

– English Phrases for Malay Visitor
(Vest-Pocket Editions, 1950

(1) *Vulture, aloof on a thermal;*
    frail flesh is a commodity
    to be scavenged.
(2) *Vulture, manipulating still-bloody bones*
    on the white sand;
    Poet, ordering the words of a beautiful sonnet
    on the bare page.

– Two Visions
(after Kokur Niznegorsky

Is this Thalia and Melpomene, or am I seein double?

– Eavesdropped
(in a Greek restaurant)

At Marsden Bay

Arid hot desert stretched here in the early
Permian Period – sand dune fossils
are pressed to a brownish bottom stratum.
A tropical saline ocean next silted
calcium and magnesium carbonates
over this bed, forming rough Magnesian
Limestone cliffs on the ledges of which
Rissa tridactyla colonizes –
an estimated four thousand pairs
that shuttle like close-packed tracer bullets
against dark sky between nests and North Sea.
The call is a shrill 'kit-e-wayke,kit-e-wayke',
also a low 'uk-uk-uk' and a plaintive
'ee-e-e-eeh, ee-e-e-eeh'.

Four boys about sixteen years old appear
in Army Stores combat-jackets, one wearing
a Balaclava with long narrow eye-slit
(such as a rapist might find advantageous),
bleached denims rolled up to mid-calf, tall laced boots
with bright polished toe-caps, pates cropped to stubble.
Three of the four are cross-eyed, all are acned.
Communication consists of bellowing
simian ululations between
each other at only a few inches range:
'Gibbo, gerrofforal getcher yaffuga',
also a low 'lookadembastabirdsmon'.

Gibbo grubs up a Magnesian Limestone
chunk and assails the ledges at random,
biffing an incubating kittiwake
full in the sternum – an audible slap.
Wings bent the wrong way, it thumps at the cliff base,
twitching, half closing an eye. Gibbo seizes

a black webbed foot and swings the lump joyously
round and round his head. It emits
a strange wheezing noise. Gibbo's pustular pal
is smacked in the face by the flung poultry, yowls,
and lobs it out into the foam. The four
gambol euphoric like drunk chimps through rock pools.
Nests are dislodged, brown-blotched shells crepitate
exuding thick rich orange embryo goo
under a hail of hurled fossilized desert
two hundred and eighty million years old.

Editorial

Being both *Uncle Chummy's Letter Box*
of *Kiddies' Column* and *Supa Scoop* besides
(*Your Headlines As They Happen*), and having the shakes
uncellophaning fags this crapulous morning,
I compose: BOY (13) CLUBS DAD TO DEATH,
CHILD (10) SCALDS GRANNY (87) TO DEATH,
SKINHEAD (14) STONES KITTIWAKES TO DEATH
AS RSPCA ASKS 'WHERE'S THE SENSE?'.

Better this afternoon after the Vaults,
I award 50 pence to Adam (9)
for this: 'Dear Uncle Chummy, I am writing
to let you know about my hamster Charlie
who's my best friend . . .' 'Keep up the good work, kiddies . . .'
(sinister dwarfs, next issue's parricides).

P.S.

The stitching new on your tiny rectangle of black,
you immerse yourself in the sad therapy of the kitchen,
withdrawing from sight when assailed by trembling and weeping
I mailed you my useless sympathy but, reticently,
withheld admiration and love for you (old-fashioned words)
who, having a grim chore to finish, get on with the job.

Hints

Find ways to make the narrative compel,
I advise students; as, in retailing this,
you might lend the issue added poignancy
by being distanced – describe the electrified
overgrown line in cool botanical terms,
white cow-parsley, *Anthriscus sylvestris*,
adding the child with anthropological
detachment, ten years old, print dress, bewildered . . .

Compelling, maybe, but mere narrative –
no moral or intellectual envoy.
Accentuate the dignified resilience
that humans, or some, are capable of still,
evinced in the sad braveness of the bereaved
whose daughter, being blind, observed no warning.

15th February

I tried to put in what I really felt.
I really tried to put in what I felt.
I really felt it – what I tried to put.
I put it really feelingly, or tried.
I felt I really tried to put it in.
What I put in I tried to really feel.
Really I felt I'd tried to put it in.
I really tried to feel what I put in.

It cost £5 in WH Smith's.
£5 it cost – WH Smith's ain't cheap.
£5 ain't cheap, not for a thing like that.
It costs, a thing like that – £5 ain't cheap.
It wasn't a cheap thing – £5 it cost.
A thing like that ain't cheap in WH Smith's.
In WH Smith's a thing like that comes costly.
A lot to pay, £5, for a thing like that.

The heart was scarlet satin, sort of stuffed.
I sort of felt it was me own heart, like.
SHE TORE THE STUFFING OUT OF THE SCARLET HEART.
I sort of stuffed and tore her sort of scarlet.
I stuffed her, like, and felt her sort of satin.
I sort of felt she'd tore out all me stuffing.
I felt her stuff like satin sort of scarlet
her stuff felt sore, torn satin whorlet scar
I liked her score felt stiffed her scar lick hurt
I tore her satin felt her stuffed her scarlet
tore out her heart stuff scarred her Satan har
I licked her stiff tore scarf her harlot hair
tied scarf tore stabbed scar whore sin sat tit star
stuffed finger scar ha ha ha ha ha ha
felt stiff scarf tight tore scarlet heart her scare
her scare stare stabbed heart scarlet feel torn mur

120

Found

Strange find – a plastic dummy from a boutique
(boots, white long thighs, pants pulled right down, a sack
over the head and torso) dumped among bins
and tumps of fetid garbage and coils of rank
sloppy dog faeces in an ill-lit alley
between the Launderette and Indian Grocer.
Incorrect diagnosis: it emits
a high-pitched rattle like Callas gargling.

Rescrutinizing 36 hours later:
what was, in sodium light, viridian,
is, in pale February sun, maroon.
About a soup-cupful remains still viscous,
black at the rim where a scabbed mongrel sniffs,
ripples taut sinew, salivates and laps.

Stedman's

I am going to write a sonnet
concerning Huntington's Chorea
from the viewpoint of a Year 2
Pharmacy student, and so
I am looking up **Chorea** in
Stedman's Medical Dictionary.

On the same page as I require,
this appears: **Choreophrasia** –
The continual repetition
of meaningless phrases.

                     I wonder
if I ought, after all, to dispatch
the pharmacist's Granny by means of
convulsions, or whether to have her
reduced to a jabbering night-hag
whose terminal speech* could be rendered
with agreeable anarchy.

* Carew, Carew, Carew, my bonny lad.
Where do we go from here? Brisk cockatoo.
Happy the man who knows not he is glue.
Which way? Which way? I *love* Jahanabad
in Spring. What drunken bard? An ironclad
means tank. My bonny lad, Carew, Carew.
From here we venture to the Portaloo
of death. Brisk cockatoo is very bad!
      I had a Polly budgie in a box.
Seagull and fox. Paisley is *not* OK.
Carew, Carew, Carew, cock, cocky, cocky.
These sweets are jolly fudgy. Chicken Pox!
These literary magazines are fey,
cock, cocky, cock. Carew. I hates a trochee!

In *A Sort of Life*, Greene remarked
(mitigating the relish with which
he observed parental distress
at the death of a ten-year-old)
'There is a splinter of ice
in the heart of a writer.'

                                I savour
the respective merits of one
kind of mayhem over another,
contentedly ponder the species
of fourteen-liner most apposite –
Petrarchan? Elizabethan?

A Recollection

She always was a great one for the pranks.
We hadn't seen her for about 5 years.
To find her in that place with all those cranks
was like one of her jokes – we laughed till our tears
unfocused her as she winked, twitched and flexed
her limbs. Then we saw that she was weeping too,
realized the reason for the high-walled, annexed,
discreetly-labelled building.

                           Sleeping through
most of the morning's 2nd Year Pharmacy,
he emerged drowsily, heard, as in a dream,
'. . . Huntington's Chorea. Though, when calmer, she
exhibited no more symptoms than extreme
involuntary twitching . . .' and recalled
the childhood visit and was newly appalled.

Ex Lab

1.

Dilute acetic
has exposed from the matrix
(limestone, Jurassic),
ischium and ilium
and interlocking pubis.

These demonstrate how
ornithischian hip-joints
differ from those of
saurischians. These bits are
believed *Scelidosaurus*.

After coffee-break
they will be made ready for
hardening resin.
        These flimsy inked surfaces
        come from the Late Holocene:

    CIRCUS STRONG-WOMAN
    CONVICTED OF MANSLAUGHTER.
    STUDENT 'GOES MISSING'
    IN AFRICAN MYSTERY.
    SKINHEAD SETS FIRE TO CAGE-BIRD.

In what was Dorset
one hundred and eighty five
million years ago,
Megalosaurus et al
flenched, flensed these bastards to mince.

2.

I am cleaning up
a piece of dinosaur shit
(Upper Cretacious,
length 20 centimetres)
that came from Mongolia.

Someone else requires
the air-abrasive machine
urgently. I stop
and peruse my copy of
a Nietzsche biography.

> Up to a point, yes.
> 'God is dead' – quite straightforward.
> But why, then, go on
> to think some mitigation
> is needed for us to face
>
> Godless cosmic dust?
> Matter just gets on with it.
> Saying 'YES to life',
> conceiving 'Übermenschen'
> is an arrogant sell-out
>
> quite as fey as 'God'.
> Anyway, Nietzsche was nuts –
> got stopped by the fuzz
> for taking off his clothing
> and bathing in a puddle.

This one matrix holds
fragments of eggshell (believed
Protoceratops –
about ninety million years
of age) and a turd fossil.

I believe in this:
no Übermenschen's remnant
(not one coprolite)
is going to be better
than this elegant stone crap.

3.

    Is Sin Sinful*ness*?
    preoccupies my pious
    colleagues over lunch.
Hydrogen and Helium –
the Original Sinners.

On this diagram
(chrono-stratigraphical),
3.6 billion
years ago may be seen as
about the start of Earth life.

    When your daughter dies
    aged ten, mown down by a train,
    console yourself thus:
    sky-pilots can forgive her
    by saying a Special Thing.

On this diagram,
the Holocene or Recent
(last ten thousand years)
is far, far, far, far too small
to register on this scale.

    You live, then you die.
    This is extremely simple.
    You live, then you die –
    no need to wear funny hats,
    no need for mumbo-jumbo.

4.

The '62 find,
Heterodontosaurus
(southern Africa,
Upper Trias), concerned me
greatly because of the *teeth*

(rather than because
Scelidosaurus had been
the earliest known
ornithischian till then)
– that almost 'canine' 'eye-tooth'!

Oozing bonhomie,
we take unwanted nick-nacks
to the Oxfam shop –
at last! the starving millions
will have a nice bite to eat!

The stomach contents
of an *Anatosaurus*
I am working on
were mummified – pine-needles
seventy million years old.

In Belfast, I read,
the craze is for hunger-strikes.
Eat your porridge up
like good little murderers
(Political Status, balls).

These five gastroliths
(stomach-stones to grind food) were
worn smooth as pool balls
by an unknown sauropod
of the Upper Jurassic.

Called to specialize
in one stratigraphical
field, I decided
the Late Holocene (*our* scene)
did not concern me greatly.

5.

At the end of the
Cretacious, a 'Great Dying'
seems to have occurred,
when half of all animal
and plant groups became extinct.

That extinction seems
to have been protracted for
a few million years;
this one, now underway, will
have reached a similar scale

in a few decades.
The hiatus resulting
in some processes
of evolution will be
extremely fascinating.

> 'SUPER-TANKA SINKS'
> (the mis-print suggests Baroque,
> fugal, cumbersome
> development of the Five-
> Seven-Five-Seven-Seven . . .).

What one enjoys most
is the manipulation
of these hapless things
at such impartial distance
to fit an imposed order.

Of course one does not
really care for the *objects*,
just the *subject*. It
is a Vulture Industry,
cashing-in on the corpses.

Vacuum, cosmic dust,
algae, rhipidistians,
internecine us
(it is a fucking good job
that it all does not matter).

From a Journal (c. 1917, in the author's possession)

My Grandfather knew Gideon Algernon Mantell
(discoverer of the Iguanodon*)*
who shewed him, in 1822, in Sussex,
those teeth! of creatures hitherto undreamed-of.

My Grandfather, in 1841,
was at the B.A.A.S. Plymouth meeting*
when Doctor (later Prof., Sir) Richard Owen
unleashed the Dinosaur on smug Victorians.

My Grandfather, a polymath, drew well,
botanized, 'Englished' Vergil, geologized.
My Grandfather was born in 1800,
Father in 1850, I myself
in 1895 . . .

He would have been
88 (but for 1917).

---

* At the 1841 Plymouth meeting of the British Association for the Advancement of Science, Owen (1804–1892), first Director of the Natural History Museum in South Kensington, suggested that *Iguanodon*, *Megalosaurus* and *Hylaeosaurus* should together be named the Dinosauria, the 'terrible lizards'.

Epithalamium

1.

. . . have great pleasure in . . .
of their daughter Crystal . . .
enclosed Gift List . . .

Dragonstraw door mat in plaited seagrass
from China.
'Tik Tok' wall clock, battery operated
quartz movement in pine frame.
'La Primula Stripe' dishwasher-proof
glazed earthenware coffee set.
Valance with neat box pleats to fit
3ft to 5ft beds (fixed by Velcro pads).
Michel Guérard's kitchen work table
with base of solid pine, including
a duckboard shelf for storage,
a knife rack and pegs for teacloths.
Boxwood pastry crimper.
'Confucius' 50% polyester,
50% cotton duvet cover.
Pine wine rack.
Pine lavatory paper holder.
Solid pine toilet seat with chrome fittings
(coated with 6 layers of polyurethane).
Iron omelette pan with curved sides.
Angus Broiler cast iron pan for steaks
and chops which combines the ease of frying
with the goodness of grilling.
'Leonardo' sofa in cream herringbone.
Honey-coloured beech bentwood rocker
with cane back and seat.
Cork ice-bucket with aluminium insert.
'Mr Toad' rattan chair from France.
Tough cotton canvas Sagbag filled
with flame-retardant polystyrene granules.

2.

The fizz is Spanish, labelled 'MEGOD CHAMPAIN'.

3.

. . . have great pleasure in . . .
will now read Greetings Cards . . .

> de da de da de da de da this wedding gift to you
> de da de da de da de da your golden years come true . . .
> All the way from America . . .
> sorry can't be there . . .
> would love to have been there . . .
> a California 'Howdy!' . . .
> de da de da de da de da all your hopes and fears
> de da de da de da de da throughout the coming years . . .
> have made their bed, must *lay* in it . . .

HA HA HA HA HA HA HA (what a riot the Best Man *is*).

4.

At their new home – 'Crimmond' (next to 'Sinatra' on one side
and 'Mon Rêve' on the other) – the presents are laid out.
They look lovely, don't they, Confucius, Leonardo and Mr Toad.

5.

Bog paper and boots are tied to their bumper.
Consummation in Calais is nothing to write home about.

Carte Postale

Dear Mum and Dad,
                 The picture shows a 'gendarme'
which means policeman. France is overrated.
For two weeks it has been wet. 9th September:
we had a 'dégustation' in the Côte
de Mâconnais and Mal got quite light-headed.
Sometimes I think it will be *too* ideal
living with Mal – it's certainly the Real
Thing. I must go now – here comes Mal.
                              Love, Crystal.

Encircling her slim waist with a fond arm,
the husband of a fortnight nibbles her throat,
would be dismayed to learn how she had hated
that first night when in Calais he had kissed all
over her, and, oh God!, how she now dreaded
each night the importunate mauve-capped swollen member.

Tryst

Me and Gib likes it here – always comes of a night,
no one else gets here, see. That's his Great-Grandad's stone.
Gassed, *he* was; got sent home from one of them *old* wars.
        Tommy, they called him.

We sprayed HARTLEPOOL WANKERS on one of them. Great!
This is the newest one – sad it is, really, it's
some little ten-year-old girlie's. Them plastic daffs
        look very nice, though.

He likes to get me down in the long weeds between
two of them marble things – I can see ivy sprout
on the cross by his head. He makes me squiggle when
        he sticks his hand up.

He works at one of them mills what makes cattle food.
He stacks the sacks. You should see them tattoos on his
arms when he flexes them. There is a big red heart
        with TRUE LOVE on it.

He runs the Packer-thing all on his own, he does.
We're saving up to get married and have a big
do like that big snob that works in our office had
        (Crystal, her name is).

I let him do what he wants – he pretends that he's
the Ripper, sometimes, and gets me down on a grave;
then what he does with his hands feels like scurrying
        rats up my T-shirt.

When we've saved up enough, we're going to wed in church.
This is alright, though – at least in the summertime.
They don't pay poor Gib much, stacking them heavy sacks
        off the conveyor.

Pacepacker

THE *PACEPACKER* NEEDS ONE OPERATOR ONLY.
PLACE EMPTY PAPER SACKS IN RACK MARKED 'SACKS',
ENSURING THEY ARE CLAMPED TIGHT WITH SPRING CLAMP.
ADJUST CONVEYORS TO CORRECT HEIGHTS. SWITCH ON.
WHEN 'START RUN' LIGHT SHOWS GREEN, PRESS 'START RUN' BUTTON.
SACKS ARE PICKED UP BY SUCKERS, STITCHED AND CONVEYED
TO ELEVATOR. ENSURE CLOTHING AND HANDS
ARE CLEAR OF CONVEYOR BELT.

                        The corrugated
rapidly-moving strip of rubber seemed
to draw the arm smoothly, unresistingly
up through the oiled steel rollers. The 'Stop Run' light
shows red. The matt belt glistens where a smear
of pink mulch, fatty lumps, flensed skin, singed hair,
is guzzled dry by plump impartial houseflies.

From 5×5×5×5×5

A dead wombat, stuffed
with contemptuous
disregard for all
anatomical
possibility,

is nailed to a beam
with a Davy lamp
and a World War 1
gas-mask and a glass
fashioned like a boot.

Utterly morose
after eight of Bass,
I review the gross
sub-species and freaks
swilling at the bar.

Those most loth to wash
breed most rapidly –
ghastly extras from
some Fellini film.
Working, as I do,

with Precambrian
specimens aged six
hundred million years
sires irreverence
for the Holocene.

*

This is a very
democratic Lounge:
Schultz lectures Logic,
Fats is a binman.
Fats gulps Mild. Schultz pays.

Schultz sips dry Vermouth.
They are both crackers.
'Conceive, if you will,
that the number 2
is blue, 3 yellow . . .'

Fats sniffs his empty,
adjusts his tweed cap,
is given more Mild.
'Conceive, if you will – '
but Fats's brain reels . . .

   4 and 5 Minstrels,
   Blue Lovely 4 Eyes,
   Tie a 3 Ribbon,
   1 Grow the Rushes,
   Bluety-Green Today,

   That Coal-4 Mammy,
   Green Man Went to Mow,
   Baby's Got 2 Eyes,
   1,1 Grass of Home
   and *Yellow Blind Mice* . . .

                    *

Agotta faggal
fagoffa lager
egg offal agarr
gag ottle og ear
a gottle of gear

   Once upon a time
   e were right famous
   ventriloquister,
   played all the Big Spots
   (the *Rex*, the *Empire*),

called isself The Great
Maestro De La Voice
(once e played before
the Lady Mayoress
of Middlesborough).

What e used to do
were make this doll speak
wi a dead queer voice –
bloody great, it were –
just like *it* talkin.

Now e gets a bit,
you know, tiddly,
gets mixed up between
what e *used* to say
on the Stage and *now*.

*

. . . in music-hall days
we could trick em with
'Gredd and gutter' – see? –
distance it was. Nah,
telly spoiled all that . . .

. . . conceive, if you will,
does red have a *size*?
Can I win a prize
on this fruit-machine
when it is not here? . . .

. . . downed a few last night,
late back, supper burnt,
she said 'You think more
of those ammonites
than of me'. (Dead right.) . . .

. . . ang on, wait a jiff:
if it isn't ere
ow the bleedin ell
canyer winna prize?
Wish I ad a pint . . .

. . . so we're in the showers
an ah held it up
shoutin 'Who's is this?
Who's got thirty-eights?'
Bluidy laugh, ye ken . . .

*

. . . 'member Johnson Clark?
used to dress up like
a posh country gent,
called his dummy Hodge.
'member 'Prof' D'Alvo? . . .

. . . I do not doubt, Fats,
that you are *au fait*
with *Logic and Art*
and the essay by
G.L. Stevenson . . .

. . . no pre-Eocene,
nor, preshumabobly,
pre-Oligoshene
speshimens exisht –
mine's another Bash . . .

. . . you know, Misha Shooo,
I ad mire you,
you are geenius
you are geen geeny
mine is pintamile . . .

. . . wusha hadda lass
wush te Goddahad
God ah wush ah had
a wee bonny lass.
God, ah *need* a lass . . .

*

Always amusing,
after a day of
defunct echinites,
to chart the advance
of the sub-species.

Dressed in the kit of
a Full Admiral,
a twerp tells jokes in
Scotch about mammae.
The ventriloquist

and Fats talk Racing.
But the ascendant
are these tattooed Skins,
LOVE on one fist and
HATE on the other,

BAD SKINS RULE in the
strobe's flash and fading.
Quite incongrous,
the highbrow Prof with
Sense of Survival

bred right out of him,
naively chats to
the juke-box on the
theme of *non-standard
possible worlds*. (Gawd.)

*

get him   in the bogs
shove his   head in it
rub his   face in shit
piss all   over him
get them   matches out

butt him   in the face
knee him   in the crotch
kick him   in the head
smash his   fuckin legs
stick one   in his nuts

posh puff   clever shite
la-de-   fuckin-da
bastard   brainy git
bleedin   college prat
we hate   puffy snobs

boot his   friggin guts
slash him   in the face
slice him   down the neck
get blood   in his eyes
knife his   nose across

set his   coat alight
squash his   other eye
looks like   cherry jam
that should   learn the twat
Bad Skins   Rule OK

*

While I was cleaning
a Silurian
matrix this morning,
someone informed me
of Schultz's mishap.

The *Railway Hotel*
is thrilled with outrage
as I sip the cure
at lunchtime. The lounge
is called 'FLYING SCOT'.

I see the man 'Fats'
and hail him, 'Ah, "Fats",
I learn with dismay
that the simians
ignited your chum.'

His response is 'Eh?'.
I repeat 'I say
it's rather hard luck
about Schultz's brush
with the sub-species.'

I notice his specs
are steaming with brine.
He wields a grubby
snot-spattered hanky,
whines 'I *loved* that man'.

*

The Formative Minds
are at it again –
exchanging sterile
platitudes, students
sip Pils, wear daft clothes.

One of them yaffles
in gormless Scotch tones
treating of ball games
and cheeky rude pranks –
he's a *fun* person.

Too much confidence,
no respectful fright
or awareness, yet,
of mortality,
too much decibel . . .

    [Here the author snatched
    up his Bic and scrawled
    on his beer mat:
    In next Saturday's
    match, regrettably,

    Jock was savagely
    tackled, losing 8
    teeth, and choking on
    1 gum-shield. He died
    in the ambulance.]

        *

. . . 5% formic
should be 'buffered' and
we use calcium
orthophosphate (that
kid from the Poly

looks unwell, and I
feel unwell, weak hearts
in both our cases,
still, what's 40 years
here or there on the

chronostratigraph?),
pint please Vi, it's from
Anachronismos,
out of time, i.e.
early position

of these things in the
stratigraphic chart
(liquor buggers us,
nathless 'Human kind
cannot bear very

much reality'),
there's no accepted
phylogenetic
relevance of shark
tooth morphology.

*

[In a quite unique
collaboration,
Author and Surgeon
today succeeded
in reviving a

hopeless cadaver
killed last Saturday
in the *Wasps'* home match.
Tipp-Ex and scalpel
joined forces to clear

a throat obstruction.
AUTHOR ADMITTED
'I ACTED IN HASTE'.
EX-SCOTTISH PATIENT
EXHUMED AS *ENGLISH*.

NATION-CHANGE DEATH-MAN.
AMBULANCEMEN PRAISED
BY REPENTANT BARD.
DOC'S DEFT KNIFE DELETES
BARD'S HASTY BIC-WORK.]

   'How are you now, Jock?'
   'Perfectly spiffing,
   actually, old thing.
   Awfully eager
   to join the Ladies . . .'

*

Photos line the walls
of the *Theatre Vaults*
signed with things like 'All
luck to Vi and staff
of the Theatre Vaults

from "Cheeky" Chump Chipps',
One is of a spent
Panto Horse and signed
'From Rick and Gordon –
always a pair for

"horseplay" '. Another
is of a man called
Simon Dee (who was,
some time ago, a
personality).

'Maestro De La Voice,
to all the bar staff;
keep your chin up!' is
curled and nicotined –
he drinks here nightly.

He is here tonight,
sixty one years old,
at this moment crouched
in the piss-stenched bogs
weeping, and weeping.

From c

*(Incongruously I plan
100 100-word units.)*

The brass plate polished wordless. Stone steps hollowed by the frightened hopeful ascending, the terrified despairing descending. (Probably between three and four months, perhaps one hundred days.) Out of the surgeries in this Georgian street, and similar streets in similar cities, some of us issue daily, bearing the ghastly prognostications. How we hate you, busy, ordinary, undying – taxi-driver, purveyor of the *Evening Star*, secretary bouncing puddings of malleable flesh. Incongruously I plan 100 100-word units. What do you expect me to do – break into bloody haiku?

> Verse is for healthy
> arty-farties. The dying
> and surgeons use prose.

*

The *Whale* is situated on the quay and is used by ferrymen and travellers calling for a quick drink before crossing. The *Colliers* is frequented by men from the pit. The fellow known as Tucker regularly attends both establishments. Perhaps he is in charge of the turnstile, the palm of his hand constantly grey from receiving pennies. Or he may be a gypsy, for he deals, apparently, in horses. He addressed me one evening in the bar of the *Whale* with importunate familiarity, remarking that I might henceforward know him as 'Char' (short for 'Charlie'?) or 'Mort' (short for 'Mortimer'?).

*

When I was a boy and read that section at the end of Book V where shipwrecked Laertides crawls under two close-growing olives, one wild one cultivated, exhausted and finds shelter, I was deeply and permanently influenced. Since then the idea of such a comforting and comfortable solitary and impregnable bower has been inseparable for me from the concept of profound sweet sleep – arfd more . . . Almost every night since that time, except when drunken or erotic diversion has rendered such conceit impracticable, I have snuggled into the warm bedlinen metamorphosing it to dry Sabaean insulating leaves, blanding approaching oblivion.

*

[He breaks down and sobs embarrassingly.] The helpless things people scream out so childishly helplessly like 'Oh please I don't want to die I don't want to die I don't *want* to die!' Well, I scream them now I DON'T *WANT* TO   OH HELP ME PLEASE I DON'T *WANT* TO DIE I. [Drivel.] Why write it? Why ever wrote any of it? Poetry all weak lies, games. Epicurus, stupid lies, that there is nothing terrible in not living. Just to stay oh living, oh, why can't I? Stupid childish helpless poor little frightened [Pusillanimous drivel.] frail poor me. Us *all*.

*

Verse unvindicable; therefore sublate *The Ballad of Tucker's Tale* (It's once he was a welterweight/And mingled with the champs/But now he isn't fit, they say,/To make arse-holes for tramps –/Kips in the Council's GRIT FOR ROADS/Fibreglass yellow bin/And Tucker's Tale's known from the *Whale*/To the *Canny Colliers Inn* . . .). During the war, Tucker's squad, randy in France, was queuing up to shag a goat. A lance-corp jumped the queue. Everyone complained, but, while the offender was on the job, his head split suddenly apart leaking grey and crimson. Sniper. Vita brevis; ars ditto.

*

Twenty of them. Should be sufficient. Comforting rattle from the brown plastic bottle. Twist of cotton wool. Label typed ONLY AS DIRECTED. Wrapped in linen in the rucksack: the decanter engraved with my initials, the eighteenth century twist-stemmed glass, the last bottle of 1894 Bual. Yapsel Bank, Hanging Brink, Ashes Hollow, Grindle Nills, Long Synalds. A good enough place to go stiff in. Quite unattended now, on hills where once my sweet wife, my dear daughter . . . (enough of that shite). Oakleymill Waterfall. Skewered by evening sun. Fat, buttery fumosity of amber decanted Madeira. Sour chalkiness of the twentieth pillule.

*

I used to pepper my poetics with sophisticated allusions to *dear* Opera and *divine* Art (one was constantly reminded of A. du C. Dubreuil's libretto for Piccinni's *Iphigenia in Tauris*; one was constantly reminded of Niccolò di Bartolomeo da Foggia's bust of a crowned woman, doubtless an allegory of the Church, from the pulpit of Ravello cathedral, ca. 1272) but suddenly these are hopelessly inadequate. Where is the European cultural significance of tubes stuck up the nose, into the veins, up the arse? A tube is stuck up my prick, and a bladder carcinoma diagnosed. One does *not* recall Piccinni.

*

My husband never once entertained the notion of transcendentalism. He regarded it as an arrogant ('arrogant humility' is a phrase he used of Buddhism, Christianity &c.), Quaternary, Hominid invention for crudely pacifying the purely physiological characteristic of Hominid cephalic capacity. He viewed the concept of theism as cowardly, conceited, unimaginative and, necessarily, at the *earliest* merely Pliocene. (His period was Precambrian, before god.)

His irascibility increased towards the end . . .

[Missionaries visited him clutching 'Good News' bibles.] You are importunate. Return to your corrugated-iron chapels and crave forgiveness of your wretched deity for disturbing the lucubrations of a bad hat.

*

[His wife and daughter tend him at home, bewildered by this revelation of his, of *all*, frailty. Special Laundry Services deal with his sheets and blankets – the soiling too foul for acceptance by normal laundries. The ambulance's arrival would be as the tumbrel's.]

Briskly efficiently deftly my daughter enters at midnight,
eases me onto my side, changes the oxygen flask.

Even formed properly, no elegiac distich can fall with
quite this sospirity: breath – out of a black mask exhaled.

None of it matters except at a purely personal level:
pain, not oblivion, hurts; as with me, so with all quarks.

*

The specialist's hands, extremely large, buff-coloured, gently manipulate my emaciated wrist, two slender bones and a knot of turquoise vein. Huge tawny thumb and forefinger tighten on a frail pulse.

It was a good ferret and almost immediately there was a rabbit in the net. The man I was with (a gyppo-looking type whose company I cultivated as a child but whose name evades me now) removed it from the nylon mesh. His hands were huge and tawny and took up the rabbit, smoothing its ruffled fur, and with soothing fondness, with infinite gentleness, affectionately snapped its neck.

*

'Quite the most maudlin man I've ever met
told me this in the lounge of the *Colliers*:
"It's many years ago now but, oh God!
I can still feel her hand rubbing my tool
as she drove slowly down the pleached-hedged lane.
She stopped the car, licked her lips, moaned, and kissėd me –
Christ!, slurping tongues like squirming warm oiled slugs –
and said 'God! I could eat you' and unzipped
my washed-out Levi's, peeled them apart and guzzled.
I'll never see her again – I've got bowel cancer." '
Run them together, set as justified prose,
the inadequately blank pentameters.

*

Now for a bit of a trip down Memory Lane. Spring breakfast, bluebells on sun-dappled gingham. A blue-hooped jug of cream, bronzed toast, Frank Cooper's. Smoked aromatic crepitating rashers. FREE!!! IN EACH PACK OF *BRAN-BREK* – A PLASTIC BUG!!! I am served a dusty handful, read the packet. *Medical Scientists are in agreement. We all need fibre, and bran is full of fibre. BRAN-BREK is full of bran, so eat BRAN-BREK. Doctors say fibreless diets cause bowel cancer. Don't take the risk – get into the BRAN-BREK habit.* What was then fear has become shitless terror.

*

I seen him once before, before – you know. I was fetching a white Welsh, 12 hands, down Grindle Nills. Between Grindle Hollow and Oakleymill there was him and his Mrs and nipper. Picnicking, they was, wine cooling in the brook. He gawped at the nag's pricked ears, large eye, dished profile, withers, mane, poll, forelock, muzzle, chin, cheek, shoulder, chest, forearm, knee, cannon, pastern, chestnut, brisket, elbow, belly, stifle, gaskin, coronet, wall of hoof, heel, fetlock, hock, thigh, buttock, dock, croup, loins, back. He knew who I was alright. 'That's a pale one ye have there, Mr Tucker' he said.

*

At the end of the Cambrian, an estimated 52% of faunal families became extinct. At the end of the Devonian, 30%. At the end of the Permian, 50%. At the end of the Triassic, 35%. At the end of the Cretacious, 26%. Last night I had to get up frequently and stagger to the bathroom at the end of the ward. Pain unendurable. Rocked back and forth on lavatory seat, groaning. At the end of the Holocene (fashionable Tropical Rain Forest reduction, fashionable Nuclear Holocaust) the percentage of faunal family extinction is likely to at least compare with Cambrian figures.

*

[He writes] *Dear* [names of his wife and child which I render 'A' and 'B' for reasons of delicacy], *I recall our Callow Hollow alfresco. Our tiny child bathing in Oakleymill Waterfall pool. A gorse sprig suspended in an eddy. We were at the best of our lives. Such happiness never recurs. Never. Golden bright little flower, sharp thorns. Spätlese cooling in the gelid spring. Later, the gipsy with that pale gelding. I will remember these things until the day I die.* [Which is the day after tomorrow. He signs his name which I render 'C' for reasons of delicacy.]

*

'Retention can give rise to undue pain;/incontinence, conversely, causes shame/and a degree of inconvenience./ Colostomies, short-circuiting the bowel/to open on the frontal abdomen,/can cause distress at first, but nothing like/the anguish that the blockage, not relieved,/would cause. Soon after surgery, it seems,/some soiling from the new colostomy/is unavoidable – patients become/aware that they can get unclean and smell . . .'

Terminal verse. Rain-pits 700000000 years old in Precambrian rock: a species evolved 696000000 years after that: a handful of stresses and punctuation: ars only as long as vita: pentameters, like colons, inadequate.

*

100 days after diagnosis, I ingest soporifics. I compose octave and first line of sestet concerning my cadaver.

> The vagrant Tucker found it, partly rotted,
> Eyes gouged by corvids, puffed blue meat, wet, stinking,
> Blown lips serrated (nibbled as if pinking-
> Shears had been at them), maggoty nose besnotted.
> From its arse pocket he took five green-spotted
> (With penicillia) £5 notes – thinking,
> Quite rightly, they'd be better used for drinking
> Bass in *The Whale* than festering, rank, clotted
>
> In [something something something] Ashes Hollow

Why? Snot, gore, filth, suppuration of the arse-gut – for these *no* metric is vindicable.

*

A regular at the *Colliers* was Head of Art at the local Poly (phoney smothie, used to take snuff). Mort bought some Itchy Powder from the *Wizard's Den* Joke Shop and one evening, when the Art bloke offered the old silver snuff-box round the bar, our hero slipped the irritant in (looked just like snuff) and handed back the antique. The offensive educationalist took no more stimulant until, on the motor-way, driving back home, he indulged, and, in the paroxysm of sneezing that ensued, collided with an oncoming articulated lorry hauling meat-and-bone-meal and was killed instantly.

*

In the Borough Library the medical dictionaries are mostly used by unfortunates looking up their maladies. The Cs are particularly well-thumbed. **CARCINAEMIA CARCINECTOMY CARCINEL-COSIS CARCINOGEN CARCINOGENESIS CARCINOGENIC CARCINOGENICITY CARCINOID CARCINOLOGY CARCI-NOLYSIN CARCINOLYSIS CARCINOLYTIC CARCINOMA-TOID CARCINOMATOPHOBIA CARCINOMATOSIS CARCI-NOMATOUS CARCINOMECTOMY CARCINOMELCOSIS CARCINOPHILLIA CARCINOPHILIC CARCINOPHOBIA CAR-CINOSARCOMA CARCINOSECTOMY CARCINOSIS CARCI-NOSTATIC CARCINOUS.** I am researching **C. ventriculi;** the woman who has just relinquished Stedman's has marked faintly in pencil **C. of uterine cervix**. We are beyond verse here. No one wants to write 'On Last Looking Into Stedman's Carcinoma'. Neverthe-less, I have invented the 13-line sonnet for unlucky people (100 words, inc. title) . . .

*

Talking shop

The three sterilizations went OK,
except for the advanced C. uterine cervix
(just my damned luck to find that) – anyway,
apart from that it all went normally.
The one in Number 2 was staggered when
I said 'We found your coil, by the way –
worked its way through the womb into the space
between the womb and stomach.' Number 3
(non compos mentis, got eight kids already)
asked me when 'it' would be alright again.
I said 'If you endeavour to avoid
sexual intercourse for about two nights . . .'
She said 'He won't wait. He *will* have his rights.'

*

His irascibility increased towards the end . . .

The sham the twee and the precious/phoney-rustic ignorant/
wield their sugary Biros/down in the safe Sticks/ensconced in the
done-up Old Wheelwright's./Poetical mawkish duff gen/where a
buzzard is 'noble' and lands/in a tree (surprise, surprise!)/to cor-
roborate some trite tenet/cum badly-observed Nature Note./Their
fauna is furry or feathery/people like you and me,/cute or nasty – a
raptor/becomes a Belfast terrorist./Bull-shit bull-shit bull-shit/of the
Plashy Fen School./Peterson, Mountfort & Hollom/write more
sense than you/bloody carpetbaggers.

*

According to Parkes ('Bereavement and mental illness', *British
Journal of Medical Psychology*, 1965, *38*, p 1), 8% of seriously distres-
sed bereaved people questioned expressed anger towards the dead
person.

'She didn't seem particularly distraught. We were just with her at
the ceremony. Suddenly she just seemed to ignore us all. "Why
have you left me, why have you gone away? Why have you left me,
why have you gone away? Why have you left me, why have you
gone away? Why have you left me, why have you gone away?" She
yelled and yelled as it went into the furnace.'

*

Muse! Sing *Phylloscopus trochiloides*!/I know it is a strange thing to recall/out of a rag-bag of experience/(rather than, say, rude goings-on with girls/or that first fright of Death – lost in thick fog/and with the tide coming in rapidly/over the mud-flats in the river mouth . . .),/but, more than early childhood or first dick,/this vagrant (which I mist-netted in youth)/incongruously gladdens my last thoughts/(and, more incongruous still, in quatorzain)./The wing formula confirmed that it was Greenish/(rather than Arctic) Warbler – longer first/and shorter second primary, of course.

*

We went to picnic up Calo Holow to have a picnic to a worto-fall and a pool the pool was very deep. I neely fell into the pool. it was very suney We had cold chicin. Daddy and Mummy lay in the gras by the streem and I played round about and had oranj juse then Mummy and daddy had some wine that was cooling in the streem. Here is a powim of it

> When I went up Calo Hill
> I took some orang I did not spill.
>
> we saw a pale grey poniy
> Daddy fel asleep by the streem

*

It's bad for us as well, you know, looking after them. Can you take any more? I can't. I'm ready to give up. What's the use? All our patients die eventually. They should do six things for their 'Death Work': (1) become aware of their impending death, (2) balance hope and fear throughout the crisis, (3) *reverse* physical survival instincts, (4) relinquish independence, (5) detach themselves from former experiences and (6) prepare 'spiritually' for death. They go through six emotional states (outlined by Kübler-Ross): (1) Denial, (2) Isolation, (3) Anger, (4) Bargaining, (5) Depression, (6) Acceptance. All, eventually. All.

*

These are the sorts of things they say, through six emotional states (outlined by Kübler-Ross), sad, self-deceiving till the last ones: 'It's just one of those things' 'I shall be out of here soon' 'I'm getting better' 'I'm feeling fine' 'It's not so bad' 'I just need a good tonic' 'Be back at work before you can say "Jack Robinson" ' 'My pneumonia's worse than my cancer'. Can you take any more? I can't. I'm ready to give up. What's the use? All our patients die eventually. Anyway, those are the things they first say, DENIAL. Next comes ISOLATION:

*

165

'You don't know how it feels' 'You can't know how it feels' 'No one understands' 'They don't tell you anything' 'I try to guess what's going on' 'On your morning rounds you seem too busy to talk' 'No one seems to realize how vital my supply of oxygen is' 'I try to hide my feelings so that the family's not too distressed' 'Don't like being on my own' 'I don't like being left alone'. Those who we have not told start to sense it – the way the nurses look at them, the way we see less and less of them . . .

*

Next comes ANGER: 'Why *me*?' 'They don't care' 'It's *my* body – they treat you like a child of 3' 'The food's lousy' 'The Quack's no good' 'A God of Love – huh!' 'The nurses is lazy' 'Why don't this happen to be the scroungers and layabouts?' 'Doctor's a fool if he thinks this treatment will work'. Next comes BARGAINING: 'If only I could be home for the daughter's wedding, I'd not care after that' 'If only I could go without pain, I wouldn't mind so much' 'If only God would spare me to do His work a little longer, wouldn't mind then.'

*

Can you take any more? I can't. I'm ready to give up. What's the use? All our patients die eventually. By now they can no longer depend on their bodies doing what, before they got ill, they thought they would do in such an eventuality – neither suicide, nor smart philosophizing. They can not conceive beforehand what it will be like. Dying nobly? My sweet arse hole. One of them wrote verse. Verse! Write verse about this: a Left Inguinal Colostomy. Shit, blood, puke and a body no longer dependable, metastases, dyspnoea . . . I shut my eyes but weep under the lids.

*

The fifth emotional state (outlined by Kübler-Ross) is that of DE-PRESSION: 'What chance have I got?' 'Not long now' 'What's the use?' 'This cancer is the end of everything' 'I'm not going to get better' 'I'm so useless now'. Last comes ACCEPTANCE: 'Thank you for all you've done' 'Dying will be a relief' 'I see things differently now' 'The wife will be so terribly lost and lonely'. These are the sorts of things they say through the six emotional states (outlined by Kübler-Ross), sad, self-deceiving till the last ones. It's bad for us as well, you know.

*

I ndian doctor examines
N ewly performed colotomy (is appalled).

T erminal case, brought into
H ere last night, won't
E ver return to Azalea Terrace.

S mall frightened old woman,
A fter anaesthetic, has dim
M emory of fainting in chip-shop (won't
E ver get out of here).

V ery smooth-looking
E xecutive-type in
R oad accident; surgeons
T ry to revive him, fail;
I n collision with lorry
C arrying meat-and-bone-meal.
A n elderly lady, supposed suicidal,
L oudly denies taking barbiturates.

C oke is shovelled
O nto the furnace by a
L oathsome old stoker who now
U nfolds the Sports Page,
M arks with an X some
N ag for the next Meeting.

Mort or *Char* (this latter pronounced 'chair' or 'care' in their infernal accents, though presumably, merely short for Charlie) possesses many katabolic anecdotes. His erstwhile leman bestowed finger-nail and teeth impressions on the mantelpiece as her distemper flourished and the burden of pain induced gripping and biting the mahogany often for hours together in the full excruciating anguish of the paroxysm. The huge firm 18-year-old malleable boobs she had let him enjoy were defiled at 42 by surgeon's scalpel and radium treatment. This rendered in catalectic tetrameters, might do for the *TLS* or other reputable literary periodical.

*

What were bronzed on Margate sands,
flopped about by trembling hands,
malleable, conical,
have become ironical.
What was cupped in palm and thumb
seres now under radium.
What was kneaded like warm dough
is where, now, malign cells grow.
What was fondled in a car
through white silk-smooth slippery bra
(Marks & Spencer, 38)
was plump cancer inchoate.

Truncation (catalexis): 'frequent in trochaic verse, where the line of complete trochaic feet tends to create monotony. The following trochaic lines exhibit t.: ''Simple maiden, void of art,/ Babbling out the very heart'' . . .' – *Princeton Encyclopedia of Poetry and Poetics* (ed. Preminger).

*

'The husband was driving. The wife, aged 23, was in the back seat. They were on the motorway. She had just been discharged from a mental institution. Without comment she took 20 barbiturates. Suddenly the young man became aware that she was comatose on the sheepskin cover. He observed the empty brown plastic phial. In panic he screeched into a Services Area and – ' 'Why had she tried to, you know?' 'Terrible fear of getting cancer, no reason to suspect it, just kept thinking she would.' (Great unvindicable idea: a 17-liner, 100-word, pentameter acrostic, first letters forming CARCINO-MATOPHOBIA.) 'Continue.'

*

'He carried her into the Ladies' Lavatory intending to make her puke up the offending drug. She could not be made to vomit. An elderly lady, unable to enter the lavatory because it was thus occupied, sat on a chair outside the cubicle. Frenzied, the young husband raced to telephone for an ambulance, leaving his spouse unconscious in the toilet. He dialled 999 on the Cafeteria phone. The Cafeteria Manageress forced him to consume three cups of hot sweet tea. Meanwhile, ambulancemen arrived, accused the seated elderly lady of ingesting barbiturates, and, despite her protestations, bore her away by stretcher.'

*

Constantly anticipating cancer/(Abdominal, lung, throat, breast, uterus,/Rectum, 'malevolent' or 'benign'), she went/ Crackers and was soon certifiable./Inside, the loopiest of all was the/Nut-doctor who prescribed barbiturates/'Only as soporifics – one per night'./ Months passed, and she accumulated 20./At length she was discharged. Her husband called/To chauffer her. 'Apparently depressed/Or meditative, otherwise OK,/Perhaps a change of scene? . . .' Motoring back,/Hopelessly fraught, she polished off the lot./Overdose verdict brought by coroner . . ./Bloody fool ambulance-wallahs kidnapped some/Idle bystander (whom they thought looked ill)/And left the suicide slumped in the bogs.

*

Ubi sunt the blue-green algae of yesteryear that by photosynthesis first oxygenated the atmosphere? In the black cherts of the Bulawayan Limestone Group dated at about three thousand one hundred million years old, in the stromatolitic sediments first noted by Macgregor, later corroborated by Schopf et al; that is where. *Ubi sunt* the good old rain-pits and ripple-marks so transiently formed about six hundred million years ago? Buried in the Late Precambrian Longmyndian matrices of this valley where I myself . . . What is 40 years here or there on the chronostratigraph? (They don't make them like that anymore.)

'They are angry with their own failing bodies . . . also apt to criticize and blame others . . . One such aggrieved . . . greatly troubled the nurses and doctors who cared for her . . . Often young nurses would leave her bedside to shed a few tears because their attempts to help her had been met by contemptuous dismissal . . . accusing those who were treating her of apathy inefficiency and callousness . . . a way of expressing her disappointment and bitterness . . . for herself and the life that seemed unfulfilled . . .' – John Hinton, *Dying*, (Penguin, 1967).

His irascibility increased towards the end . . .
'Piss off, Sky Pilot', I whisper in the Padre's ear.

*

(Not just me, but all of us in the same vertical column. I pass the same hopeless pyjamad cases in ghastly contraptions daily. In the snot-green corridors daily the covered trolleys are shunted. Daily the meat-wagons swing through the gates braying, pulsing blue light, their burdens already history scraped off the Tarmac. Daily and nightly the trolleys the trolleys the trolleys jingle like gently shaken tambourines as they hasten with cargoes of shiny stainless-steel kidney-shaped bowls and glinting clamps, needles and blades and forceps, acres of soft white lint to one or another and finally all.)

*

The doctor had told me but not him. One evening he was struggling
with a pile of papers – administrative stuff, to do with the conference
on Early Precambrian Stromatolite Morphology and Taxonomy –
when he slumped into his seat, exhausted by the simple exertion. I
touched his arm and said (I hear my voice and its slight echo from
the sparsely furnished study as if it is played back to me on tape) 'Oh
my darling, you should not trouble with anything unessential; you
see, you are dying.' He simply replied 'I understand' and replaced
the documents in the mahogany bureau.

*

Newsflash, their women writhe unconsolable in the dirt of Ulster
and the Holy Land. They are not actresses; that is how they really
feel. How I feel also, my cancerous husband. Newsflash after
newsflash, their women writhe unconsolable in the dirt of Ulster
and the Holy Land. They are not actresses; that is how they really
feel. How I feel also, my cancerous husband. Newsflash after
newsflash after stinking newsflash, their women writhe unconsol-
able in the dirt of Ulster and the Holy Land. They are not actresses;
that is how they really feel. How I feel also, my cancerous husband.

*

(Not just me, but the public clocks in the cities are fucked-up –/the Building Society one, the one on the Bank,/the one on the Town Hall, the one at the Station, all stopped/at a hopeless time and whereas when I was a child/they were constants to be relied on, now the resources/and requisite knowledge to fix them are gone. And this isn't/some crusty superannuated old Colonel/lamenting, saying 'Of course, it was all fields then . . .',/but me, as my cardio-whatsit ticks limply, observing/the clocks all knackered, whereas they used not to be.)

*

Char helped the Undertaker once. The passenger had lived alone in a cottage with a couple of dogs. It sat rigid in an armchair, sap-green translucent glaze over the cheekbones. Char smoothed the back of his finger gently over the brow (the skin was unpliable, cool, waxen) then leered, and between thumb and grimy palm grasped the yellow lardy chin and shook it with hatred. The grey tongue lolled. One of the dogs, a trembling whippet, mounted the cadaver's bare knee, ejaculating after several minutes' rut. Char pocketed £25 from the mantelpiece, lowered the stiff into its fibre-glass vessel.

*

When I worked with Schopf on the Huntsman Quarry stromato-lites, we concluded that the Bulawayan deposit could be interpreted as placing a minimum age (ca 3100000000 yrs) on the origin of cyanophycean algae, of the filamentous habit, and of integrated biological communities of procaryotic micro-organisms presumably including producers (blue-green algae), reducers (aerobic and anaerobic bacteria) and consumers (bacteria, predatory by absorption). This interpretation was supported by the occurrence of filamentous and unicellular alga-like and bacterium-like microfossils in other Early Precambrian sediments. I am dying (Carcinoma ventriculi) but what is 40 years here or there on the chronostratigraph?

*

I should have started my sabbatical
but now it is impossible. Six weeks
ago they took the part-time employee,
hired to replace me, into hospital,
opened him up and said he had three months
before he pegged out – cancerous guts. They fetched
some out, but found too much inside.

                             He keeps
a sort of journal, so they say, in which
he chronicles his death in the 3rd Person,
partly in prose, part verse, peculiar, hey?
He's only young-ish too. So that's the end
of my sabbatical – I'm pretty miffed
(nor, I suppose, is he too chuffed about it).

*

No verse is|adequate.||Most of us|in this ward
will not get|out again.||This poor sod|next to me
will be dead|in a month.||He is young,|has not been
married long,|is afraid||(so am I,|so am I).
When his wife|visits him||(every day,|every day)
he takes hold|of her sleeve,||clutches her|savagely
screaming 'Please,|get me well!||Dear sweet God,|make me well!'
Quasi sham|tétramètre,|| sub Corneille,|sub Racine,
is too grand,|is too weak,||for this slow|tragedy,
screaming 'Please,|get me well!||Dear sweet God,|make me well!'

*

Wheeled back to bed. I try to lift my arms. Cannot. The Romany
performs with his mysterious poles. I am told to get some sleep.
Staff Nurse calls the stretcher-blankets 'cuddlies'. Throat rusk-dry.
I am uncomfortable but unable to turn onto my side. Eventually I
heave myself onto my side . . . At an unknown time tea is brought.
I feel sick. They wash my face and hands. The rubber under the
sheets makes me sweat. BRAN-BREK is proffered. The surgeon who
performed it appears. A pleasant, worried Sikh. He is afraid of what
I am going to ask.

*

Not just me, but also, out there, the cities whose shit/surges into
the sea in tsunamis,/and Shopping Precincts whose shit of canines
and rolling/Coke tins and paper and fag-ends and polystyrene/chip-
trays and plastic chip-forks rattle in bleak winds,/and those who
wash least, breed most, to all of us, all,/a shoddy incontrovertible
burial in shit./

This isn't some crusty Colonel (retired) lamenting/'Of course it was
all fields then, you see, in those days . . .',/but me, me, suppurating
to death,/not just on my own but with us all, with us all.)

*

Some of us benefit from a self-shielding shunning of awful
thoughts about dying and, worse, physical pain at the end.

Nevertheless we are conscious of being falsely deluding,
when we say jauntily 'Oh! I shall be out of here soon!'

Adequate realization of what is truly awaiting
does not prevent us from this: never admitting we *know*.

Even though sometimes I talk about this abdominal cancer,
my mental ease demands lies, comfort of make-believe games –

Such as this one that I play now in distich, almost pretending
verse has validity. No. Verse is fuck-all use here, now.

*

The meat-waggon comes for another unfortunate. Borne out o
Azalea Terrace, the disgusting old victim looks glum, stunnec
stupid, no longer working properly. There is bright pink sp
dribbling onto the clean black sleeve of an ambulance man wh
holds one end of a stainless steel wheelchair thing and cradles th
nasty head. Cold metallic joints lock slickly. A disinfectant whif
One-way window. Blue pulse. Sitting on a yellow fibre-glass roac
grit bunker, the Mad Tramp pulls at a whisky bottle (White Horse
and guffaws a perfect pentameter:

Hă Há|hă há|hă há|hă há|hă há.

*

Evolution (including mass faunal extinction, at the end of th
Cambrian, Holocene &c.) is what happens – not what shoulc
according to *sapiens* interpretations, happen.

It seems to be the greatest pain I've known in my life. Respiratio
fails because of it, sweat streams, I think (I *hope*) I'll faint under i
Members of hospital staff are conditioned to pay no heed to (nc
administer sufficient analgesics for) such excruciation. I feel menta
as well as physical strain and inadequacy.

None of it *matters* (except at a purely personal level). Pain, nc
oblivion, hurts. As with me, so with all quarks.

*

He breaks down and sobs embarrassingly.] Oh! I shall miss you so. Why has it happened? Why has stuff inside me suddenly gone terribly wrong? I don't think I'm afraid of not *being* anymore but so terribly terribly frightened of not being *with you*. And the child; no more playing catch with that large red-and-blue-spotted plastic ball. Never. Anymore. She called it Mr Spotty. [Mawkish drivel.] I can't be brave tonight. Oh my darling, help me! Look after me! Can't be brave or consoled by philosophy or by po – would willingly never have written anything if *only*

*

He had just died and screens surrounded the bed but the porter had not had opportunity to remove the body. I arrived at Visiting Hour when all the nurses were busy and unable to intercept me. I went straight to the screened bed and, employing a funny voice (derived from Donald Duck) which we had developed during our years of marriage for times of particular playfulness, addressed the occupant through the plastic panel thus: 'Howsqush my dearsqush old drake thisqush eveningsqush?'. Visitors at adjacent beds regarded me patronizingly. Then I bobbed my head round the screen and con- fronted the shroud.

*

[He breaks down and sobs embarrassingly.] I keep thinking *if only*
Oh, help me! And I can't believe it – that I am really going t
        It is as if I were just writing about someone else d – just as
it were yet another of the things about those poor *other* people that
write (*used* to write) about. Why am I writing about it? Can't be brav
tonight. [Drivel.] Oh, my darling, if only I could stay here not go no
go not die! [Drivel.] Oh, I shall miss you so [Drivel.] terribly! terribly
Oh my dear darl [&c.]

                              *

Now I envisage the lachrymose mourning of my wife who loved me
there is the clearing of drawers, folding of vacated clothes.

'Here is the T-shirt and here are the denims he wore in the summe
well, he was then, and robust. Here is the green and red shirt

worn, I remember, as we walked together last year on his birthday
Here are the shoes he last wore – still in the treads of one heel

dry worms of mud and dead bracken remain from that day on
                                        Long Synalds.'
Empty, amorphous and cold, blue tubes of Levi's. She weeps.

                              *

'They feel worthlessness and emptiness without the deceased. "Now I am nothing." "Feel empty inside." (Loss of self-esteem.) They wish to believe the deceased is not dead. Happy and sad memories of the deceased. Concern for the deceased's missing life-enjoyment. "I am here not deserving to be alive while he is dead, unable to enjoy this lovely day." (Guilt.) "It is a dream; he'll be back tomorrow." (Need to deny the loss.) "I've disposed of his clothing." (Demonstrates *either* ability to relinquish bond to the deceased *or* compulsion to rid themselves of the pain which that clothing evokes.)'

*

Here are some of the things you'll need if it takes place at home: bed-care utensil set (inc. denture cup, kidney basin, bed pan &c.), large sheet of plastic, rented wheelchair, box of flexible drinking-straws, one bag disposable bed pads (the incontinent will use considerably more), large size disposable diapers (several boxes), thermometer, one bottle ethyl alcohol, cotton balls, lubricant, commode, a great many spare undersheets, six wash-cloths.

Each nostril must be cleaned with a twist of tissue or cotton wool. Eyelids should be swabbed with wool swabs and warm normal saline, especially in the morning.

*

181

[He writes] *Dear* [names of the Managing Director and one of the editors of his publishers], *I am irritated to learn that I shall soon be dead. You will be irritated to learn that by then I shall have completed a final book. This epistle constitutes one of its 100 sections. I shall be dead by the time you receive this typescript. Set it in the old way – in Tedious Acrimonious roman and Poppa-Piccolino italic on hand-deckled ipecacuanha leaf bound in reversed brushed papoose.* [He signs his name.]

PS. Seriously, though, my wife will deal with proof correction.

*

[*Ubi sunt* the beldam who collapsed in Pride of Place, the micro-palaeontologist with C. ventriculi, the hag carried off by ambulance from Azalea Terrace, the loon barbiturate ingester, the Master of the 100 100-Word Units, the C3 sniper victim, the lady with C. uterine cervix, the lady with breast cancer, the gent with bladder ditto, Epicurus, the jet-set exec-looking Head of Fine Art (snuff sternutator), the leucotomized folk-singer (singin whack for my diddle), &c[n]? All planted, at the time of going to press. Some feared oblivion; most feared pain. Poor frail dear frightened little vulnerable creatures.]

*

I have administered anti-emetics and stool softeners and allowed him to eat and drink. He seems free of pain and nausea but vomits periodically whilst remaining comfortable. He describes the sensation as being similar to defecating – relieving an uncomfortable fullness. I treat his ascites with the insertion of a LeVeen shunt. Unfortunately he has developed fungating growths and draining fistulae. Particularly troublesome are the fistulae in the perianal area originating from the urinary and intestinal tracts. I performed Turnbull's Diverting Loop Transverse Colostomy (see *Current Surgical Techniques*, Schering, 1978). Bloody oozing, odour and haemorrhage occur from his decubitus ulcers.

*

My fistulae ooze blood and stink,
I vomit puce spawn in the sink,
diarrhoea is exuded.
Do not be deluded:
mortality's worse than you think.

You find the Limerick inapposite? Try the pretty Choriamb?

Bed-sores without; swarm-cells within.
Rancified puke speckles my sheets.
Faeces spurt out quite uncontrolled
into my bed, foetid and warm.
Vomit of blood tasting of brass,
streaked with green veins, splatters my face.

In vomiting, the glottis closes, the soft palate rises and the abdominal muscles contract, expelling the stomach contents. In nausea, the stomach relaxes and there is reverse peristalsis in the duodenum.

*

183

It is not as one can imagine beforehand. Dysgneusia (an altered sense of taste occasionally occurring in cases of advanced malignancy) prevents my savouring the cigar-box-spiciness, deep, round fruitiness of the brick-red luscious '61 *Cheval Blanc*, the fat, buttery cooked, caramel-sweet-nuttiness of the 1894 Bual.

'He is a patient with dysgneusia and severe dysphagia and a fairly advanced tumour for whom adequate hydration and nutrition are maintained by frequent small feedings of liquids. The insertion of an intraluminal esophageal tube is considered helpful. The dysphagia is due to an obstruction in the esophagus and hypopharynx.'

*

An absorbent pad placed under the corner of the mouth at night will prevent dribbling causing wetness and discomfort. Ice may help stimulate muscle movement. Pass an ice cube from the corner of his mouth towards the ear, then dry the skin. It may help to wipe an ice cube round his lips, then dry them. (One of them had some movement in the eyelids and was able to blink Morse messages. Phrase questions to receive very simple answers, e.g: 'There is jelly and ice cream or egg custard – would you like jelly and ice cream?' Pyjamas should be absorbent.

*

In Ashes Valley this evening I crawl under
        sheltering bushes
Joined at the same stock, so close together they
        let no light through them
And where no rain can pelt through their meshed roof, so
        knitted together
One with the other they grow. And I merge myself
        into the brown husks.
Weakly I rake together a litter from
        dry leaves that lie here
Deeply sufficient to succour two or
        three if they wanted
Warmth against Winter however malicious the
        elements' onslaughts.
Thus do I bury me closely with leaf-mould and
        wait for Athene's
Soft anaesthetic, benign soporific, ar-
        cane analgesic . . .

*

. . . by a vagrant.
There was an empty
bottle, and, oddly,
a glass and decanter
– rather posh ones.
There was no money.
Oh, yes, and this
page of note-pad . . .

*final lines of the sestet
of the final Petrarchan.
'Hollow' forms the first
c. I require dcdee. 'Follow'
could be the second c.*

*No. Something more prosy
for this job. The morphine,
the colostomy – fuck-all
there to justify lyric/metre.
But some structure still?
Why? Dignity? – bollocks.*

*But some structure still,
incongruously . . .*

*100 units each of 100 words.
How about that? Neat. One unit
per day for 100 final days.*

*

Precambrian sub-division *Longmyndian*, ca. 600 million yrs, old. An
individual Holocene *H. sapiens* with terminal pathogen. The co-
incidence of these two, thus: approaching oblivion (by ingestion or
soporifics), *H. sap.* picks up, from scree in Ashes Hollow, a sample
of rock imprinted with 600-million-year-old rain-pits. Suddenly,
alas, the subtle grafting of a cdcdee Spenserian sestet onto an
abbaabba Petrarchan octave does not matter. Vita b.; ars b. Nor does
the Precambrian sub-division *Longmyndian*, ca. 600 million yrs. old,
nor Holocene *H. sap* with terminal &c., nor the *conception* of its not
mattering, nor

*

(The suicide is untrue. Bodily weakness prevents my moving from the bed. The dismay to my wife and child which suicide would occasion renders such a course untenable. They would interpret my self-destruction as failure on their part to nurse me properly. Conversely, the grief my daily decline causes them is difficult for me to bear. If I could only end the terrible work and unpleasantness I cause them . . . But bodily weakness prevents my moving from the bed. Shit gushes unbidden from the artificial anus on my abdomen. My wife patiently washes my faece-besmirched pyjamas, for *prosaic* love.)

From UKULELE MUSIC

BOOK 1

UKULELE MUSIC

Dear sir,

I come in this morning instead of tomorrow as I have to take ~~Budige bugdie~~ Bird to the Vets, as he got out of cage door for the first time, By <u>accident</u>. As I was putting seed in. & taking out sand sheet. He went mad. & banged himself against THE wall. & fell down on to the Magic coal fire. got jammed in the back of coal effect. Broken leg and side of his body awfull state. he is in. good job fire was not on.

faithly Viv

p.S. could you oblige the next weeks money this wk. be in tomorrow Morning, Only the Capting which I chars for tuesdays has let me off this Tues but has PAID yrs Viv

*

*Few atrocities
of which* H. sap. *can conceive
remain unfulfilled*

'They must have been about 17/18, possibly 19:
one, tattooed on his hand MAM; one, tattooed on his arm LOVE.

One of them grabbed at my handbag but I just belted him with it, caught him one under the ear, then I yelled "Somebody, help!"

Even although it was lunchtime and several people were watching nobody wanted to know. Two women just walked right past.'

She had been pushing her 8-month-old, Sharen-Jayne, in the buggy.
Now the kid started to scrawk; one of our heroes smirked, spat,

fondled the empty pint bottle he had in his hand and then smashed
it
on an adjacent brick wall, held the bits to the child's throat.

'I said "Hurt me if you like but don't injure the innocent baby –
it can't defend itself, see? Don't do it don't do it *please*!"

He said "If I do the baby I'll get what I want, so I'll cut it."
He shoved the glass in her cheek; twisted the jagged edge in.

He told me "This is how we earn our living, this and the dole like."
Then he just wiggled the sharp, smashed slivers into her eye.'

Promptly the mother gave over her golden wedding-ring, also
three pounds in cash and a watch (silver, engraved 'My True Love'),

but the attackers slashed Sharen twice more – in the mouth, and a
deep cut
neatly round one chubby knee. Then they strolled leisurely off.

'Sharen was screaming and bleeding a lot and I thought they had
killed her.'
C.I.D. officers say 'This is a callous assault . . .'

*

Dear Sir,

*will finish of your hoovering and such tomorrow as my hand is still bad, my
right one. As last wk. there is a lady two doors off me has a bitch and a little
boy over the road had been playing with it. and since then where all the dogs
come from I do not know. But one of them had pinned the boy against the
wall. I ran out with a hand full of pepper to throw at the dogs face. I throw it.
but it had bit me in the hand. just above my right thumb where the bone is. I
ran after the dog. with a whitening brush also and I fell also over the fence.
bruised my knee's. But my knee is alright. My hand I have sufferd. The dog
got put down to sleep. I have been to Hospitle But I heard later. that another
dog had pinned the same boy he is only four yrs old. and MARLD him in the
face and eyes he has had 5 stitches across his left eye. The other dog also had*

192

to be put down to sleep I tell you it has been awfull over there with the dogs. The woman who the bitch belongs to, had forgotten she had left her kitchen window open One of the dogs had jump in through the window. her Husband had delt with the dog. But slammed the kitchen window and all of the glass had fallen out in pieces. (It is awfull. when the little girls are about.) There mothers have to keep them in. or take them with them. the pain is going all the way up my arm. I have had a TECNAS. you know, a little RED CARD.

YRS Viv.

*

Stubbornly, Taffs, at their damn-fool anachronistic eisteddfods, still, with this breach in the hull, twang (ineffectual lyres).

Mercury falls, it's no go, and the pink geraniums shrivel: ceilidh and Old Viennese drone as the packet goes down.

When all the cities were felled by the pongoid subspecies in them (Belfast, Jerusalem, Brum., Liverpool, Beirut) and when

blood-swilling (Allah is wonderful) Middle-East Yahoos had
purchased
nuclear hardware, he found distich the only form apt.

Too Many Of Us and Dwindled Resources and War had undone us. Matter impartially throve (quark, strangeness, charm) not as *us*.

Sing in Your Bath if You Want to Seem Sexy and **Blood-Bath in Jordan**
vie for front page in the tabs. Doh ray me fah soh lah te

*

193

well, Sir,

Only, the Capting has said I was not really wanted so I have gone to you instead. only. You are not here as you know. So have let myself in with spare key but he has PAY me just the same as he is kind old man with heart of gold etc. and has told me how underneath. and he has seen it with OWN eyes so knows it is true. where I thought it was just Underground Car Park ect. under ~~Civic~~ Civet Centre is not just Car Park but bunk for FALL if there is trouble, that sometimes seems likely with uSA and russiens with there bomb warfair. But what can you do? nothing and he say there are SARDINES stored in there for after siren, with DRINK. so we are all prepared thank God. But what I want to know is when you vote the different Goverments do NOT do what you ask do they? Because I want NO TROUBLE but it seems no difference what you want the Rulers just do a DIFFERENT THING. So you can only keep CHEERFUL and keep trying your best. sir. for Exsample I have done the floors but their is one of Yr writings there that ALAS is swept in the Hoover bag, and I got it out all right but is VERY twisted with the thing that BEATS as SWEEPS as CLEANS the one about a Piano and a Man AND woman that I think is DIRTY but it takes all sorts and did you REALLY work at such a club in uSA? I never knew you had been there but I would not want sardines ALL THE TIME who would? noone. but it would be <u>emergency</u> like in the last one where it was tin sheeting. But now they are on the streets the ARMY against thugs and Mugers as that is where the REAL war is on NOW, cities in 2 halfs with police and army and nice folks against dirty animals, so may HAVE to go DOWN soon for THAT war. But I have throw it away, the poetry writing on the Piano at top of kitchin bin VERY TOP if you want it back.

and Oblige Viv.

*

Beetrooty colonels explain to the Lounge Bar how, in the 'Last Show',

they had a marvellous time, and how we need a new war

if we are going to get this Great Country back on its feet, sir
(also all beards should be shaved: also the Dole should be stopped).

Life still goes on and *It isn't the end of the world* (the child-soothing
platitudes weaken now Cruise proves them potentially false).

Lieder's no art against these sorry times (anguished Paramour
likens
mountainy crags and a crow to the flint heart of his Frau).

*

Oh sir,

*only I havnt known. which way to TURN since the Funeral. It was the
sisters youngest such a good lad too and only ten it seems wrong. somehow,
and they would play in the streets though they was told often enough GOD
only knows. So it was a bus when they was playing football and the poor little
mite had gone when they got him. to the Hospitle so that is why I didnt' come
for 3 days but was in this morning and hope you find this note behind the tea
pot and with thanks for the new Polish which have done the desk and chairs
with. My oldest Trevor has been TOWER OF strenth since tragdy but will
get those tatoos just like his DAD in that way just last week got MAM done
on his hand which is nice he is a good lad to his Mother and a Tower. So can I
have last weeks moneys though I did not come and not have money next week
instead. Only the flowers which was a cross of pink flowers. very nicely
done. do cost such a lot not that you bigrudge it do you when its your own
Sisters youngest? So if you could leave it buy the dusters and furnature wax
it will be fine tomorrow.*

Obliged, Viv.

*PS we take her to the zoo next weekend to take her out of herself. the sister. as
it will be a nice change our Trevor says.*

*

'Them animals is disgusting.'

In London Zoo is a large flat painted Disneyesque lion
sporting a circular hole cut where the face ought to be.

On its reverse is a step upon which the visitor stands and
puts his own face through the hole – so that he may be thus
snapped.

So, the resultant photograph shows the face of a friend or
relative grinning like mad out of a leonine frame.

This seems to be a very popular piece of equipment –
Arabs in nightshirts and Japs queue with Jews. Polaroids click.

Tabloids blown underfoot headline a couple of global débâcles.
Gran, from the lion's mouth, leers: toothless, cadaverous, blithe.

Oh it is very funny to put your head through the facial
orifice of a joke lion – races and creeds are agreed.

Down the old Monkey House there is a *Cercopithecus* wanking
and a baboon (with its thumb stuck up its arse) to revile.

*

*Dear Sir didnt come in yesterday as planned as I lost key and how it
happened was this. that we went to zoo with sister and the children which
was the sister lost her youngest. And while we was throwing a ten pence for
luck onto back of Allergator corcodile which is in Tropical House it must have
fell from my purse. Everyone throws money for luck onto back of this Reptile
and his pool is FULL of two P ten P and 5P pieces which bring GOOD
LUCK to thrower. So had to go yesterday to see if the keeper had found it. he
had and said they empty pool every month and spend money. It buys keepers
there beer he says they get POUNDS so I got key back that is why I am here
today instead but unfortunatly have by ACCIDENT spoilt one of your
papers with poetry on it that was on yr desk as I threw it on the Parkray by
mistake. and hope this is no inconvenience or can you do another one instead?
Sister much better since outing but oldest boy Trev in trouble with police*

who came last night to house but I dont believe it as he is a good boy. But she is perking up a bit now and was cheerful at weekend and my boy took a Poloid Photo of her with head through a LION which was V. funny and makes her laugh which is good for her. Police say he has mugged but it canot be as he is GOOD BOY.

faithly VIV. p.s. worse things happen at SEA!

*

'Life is too black as he paints it' and 'Reading's nastiness sometimes seems a bit over the top' thinks a review – so does *he*.

Too black and over the top, though, is what the Actual often happens to be, I'm afraid. He don't *invent* it, you know.

Take, for example, some snippets from last week's dailies before
they're
screwed up to light the Parkray: Birmingham, March '83,

on her allotment in King's Heath, picking daffodils, Dr
Dorris McCutcheon (retired) pauses to look at her veg.

Dr McCutcheon (aged 81) does not know that behind her,
Dennis (aged 36) lurks, clutching an old iron bar.

Unemployed labourer Dennis Bowering sneaks up behind her,
bashes her over the head – jaw, nose and cheek are smashed-in.

Dennis then drags her until he has got her into the tool-shed,
strikes her again and again, there is a sexual assault,

also a watch and some money worth less than ten pounds are stolen.
Is an appalling offence . . .' Bowering is told by the Judge.

Amateur frogmen discover a pair of human legs buried
Mafia-style in cement, deep in an Austrian lake.

Smugly, Americans rail over KA 007;
angrily, Moscow retorts. Hokkaido fishermen find

five human bits of meat, one faceless limbless female Caucasian,
shirts, empty briefcases, shoes, fragments of little child's coat,

pieces of movable section of wing of a 747,
one piece of human back flesh (in salmon-fishermen's nets),

one headless human too mangled to ascertain what the sex is.
USA/USSR butcher a Boeing like chess

(probably civil jumbos *are* used for Intelligence business;
pity the poor sods on board don't have the chance to opt out).

Sexual outrage on woman of 88 robbed of her savings.
Finger found stuck on barbed wire. Too black and over the top.

Clearly we no longer hold *H. sapiens* in great reverence
(which situation, alas, no elegiacs can fix).

What do they think they're playing at, then, these Poetry Wallahs?
Grub St. reviewing its own lame valedictory bunk.

*

dear Sir,

well I have hooverd and wax pollish the desk so I will collect money
tomorrow. There is trouble on our block since my Tom plays the bones to
tunes of George Formby and was due to give a TURN at the club tonight but
was paralitic last night and WOULD try to practise and of course one of
them. the bones. went over next door and the woman there that has the bitch
that MARLD the child well her bitch grabs the bone but my Tom shouts
abuse and. of course the outcome is there is a window broke. Which the man
next door have only just mended after the last trouble, so we will see how it
goes tonight at the Club he does that one he played his Youkerlaylie as the
Ship Went down. and I know how He felt, because it is the same with my
eldest Trevor who is REPRIMANDED IN CUSTARDY as the policeman

put it who is a nice man but I know my lad is innerscent of that awful thing they say he done. But these things are sent to TRY Us as my Man says and I hope he plays his bones well tonight. just like he did that year we were in the T.V. show Mr and Mrs, did you know we were in it? yes in Llandudno and he entertained the crowds they were in stitches when the ONE MAN BAND never turned up. so I have used up all the Johnsons Wax again so please oblige, We all have problems even the different Parlerments, also the police Forces. as well as me, and you with Yr writings

Viv, P.S. we can only carry on the best we can manage

Was one time anchored in forty
fathom near unto the shore
of Mascarenhas Island.
Landed, we found blue pigeons
so tame as to suffer us
to capture them by our hands
so that we killed and roasted
above two hundred the first day.
Also we took many others –
grey paraquets, wild geese
and penguins (which last hath but stumps
for wings, so cannot fly).
Most entertaining to catch
a paraquet and make it
cry aloud till the rest
of its kind flocked round it and thus
enabled themselves to be caught.
Twenty five turtle, lying
under one tree, was taken.

On then to St. Mary's Island,
where we careened, and thence
stood for the Straights of Sunda.

At 5° 30′
south of the line, the alarm
'Fire!' was raised – the steward
had gone below for brandy,
thrust candle into the hole
of a cask on the tier above
whence he drew his spirits, and when
removing his candle, a spark
had fell from the wick down the bung,
igniting the spirit. He poured
water unto the cask,
by which we had thought to choke it.

But the flames, reviving, blew out
the cask ends, when the fire

reached to a heap of coals
stowed there, which, lighted, gave off
a thick sulphureous smoke
thwarting attempts to extinguish it.

In this emergency
I appealed to the supercargo
to cast overboard all powder.
But (stubborn, arrogant, greedy,
as so many of his class)
he refused. Says he 'To throw
our powder away is to risk
attack from our enemies'.

Meantime the rage of the fire
augmented more and more.
We scuttled decks that greater
floods of water could be
got into ye hold, but all
attempts proved vain.

                 I resolved
to summon the carpenters
with augers to bore the hull
that water might enter below
and quench the flames.

                But our oil
ignited then, d'ye see?,
and with sixty five good men
I stood on deck by the main
hatchway receiving buckets
when the powder, 300 kegs,
was reached.

             The vessel blew up
into the air with one hundred
and nineteen souls: a moment

afterwards, not one single
human being was seen:
believing myself to be launched
into eternity,
I cried out aloud for Mercy.

Some slender remnant of life
and resolution still lurked
in my heart. I gained the wreck,
as was gone to a thousand pieces,
clung to a yard.

                    The long-boat,
got off afore the explosion
by a deserting faction,
now, in the very worst
of my extremity,
ran to the place with all speed,
whereat the trumpeter
threw out a line by which
I obtained that frail haven
of temporary ease,
and hymned being simply extant.

                    *

Cast up, one time, wrecked,
on bleak Patagonia
out of the Wager, Indiaman,
Commodore Anson's squadron.
Six years, afore we reached home.

Only food, shellfish and raw seal –
as we managed to stone unto death
or found dead, raw, rank, rotted.

Reduced thus to misery,
and so emaciated,
we scarce resembled mankind.

At nights in hail and snow
with naught but open beach
to lay down upon in order
to procure a little rest –
oftentimes having to pull off
the few rags I was left wearing,
it being impossible
to sleep with them on for the vermin
as by that time swarmed about them;
albeit, I often removed
my sark and, laying it down
on a boulder, beat it hard
with an huge stone, hoping to slay
an hundred of them at once,
for it were endless work
to pick them off one by one.
What we suffered from this
was worse even than the hunger.
But we were cleanly compared
of our captain, for I could compare
his body to nothing more like
an ant hill, so many thousand
of vermin crawling over it;
for he were past attempting
to rid himself in the least
of this torment, as he had quite
lost himself, not recollecting
our names that were about him,
nor his own. His beard as long
as an hermit's: that and his face
being besmirched of filth
from having been long accustomed
himself to sleep on a bag
in which he kept stinking seal meat
(which prudent measure he took
to prevent our getting at it
as he slept). His legs swelled huge
as mill-posts, whilst his torso
was as a skin packet of bones –

and upon bleached seal bones he played
hour after hour in uncanny
tattoo as to harmonize
with a wordless mindless dirge
as he moithered, moithered, moithered,
weird, xysterical airs,
yea, even unto the end.

*

Sailed one time aboard
trawler the Lucky Dragon,
crew o' 23,
hundred miles off Bikini,
in the March of '54.

Tars was all below
down in the a'ter-cabin;
crew man, Suzuki,
run abaft a-hollering
'The sun rises in the West!'

Hands mustered on deck,
saw, to larboard, a fireball,
like a rainbow brand,
rise up from ye horizon,
silent, that was the queer thing.

Minutes passed; the blast
suddenly shook the ocean,
shuddered our whole hulk,
hands was belayed with affright,
none, howsomdever, hurt (*then*).

But the skies turned *strange* –
misty wi' weird white ashes
as *swirled*, d'ye see?,
down onto decks, men, rigging . . .
That ash made us ill (*later*).

*

Since I have so often felt
the malignant influence
of the stars presiding over
the seas, and by adverse fortune
lost all the wealth which, with such
trouble and care, I amassed,
it has been no source of pleasure
recalling to memory
the disasters that have assailed us.

Still, as a singer a song
or an old player an air,
I am impelled to convey
salt observations, a tar's
chantey habit, d'ye see?

I know not whether we've bid
adieu to the sea, or whether
we shall set forth again
where we have known such mischief;
whether traverse the ocean
in quest of a little wealth;
or rest in quiet and consume
what our relations have left us.

Our strange propensity
to undertake voyages,
alike to that of gaming –
whatever adversity
befalls us, we trust, at length,
prosperity shall o'ertake us,
therefore continue to play.

So with us at sea,
for, whatever calamity
we meet with, we hope for some
chance opportunity
to indemnify our losses.

And shall it, now, be counted
as ye dignified defiance
in us towards our fateful
merciless element,
or gull naiveté,
cousin to recklessness,
that, e'en in pitching Gulphward,
our salt kind brings forth chanteys?

Who would have thought it Sir, actually putting ME in a WRITING!
me and the Capting and ALL. What a turn up for the books.

Only, I must say I do not know HOW them people in poems
manage to say what they want — you know, in funny short lines,

or like what YOU do with them ones of yours sir, made of two lines like.
Still, when you're USED to it like, then you can speak natural.

Only, the newspaper man said that you was TRYING to sound like
low classes voices and that, only you wasn't no good —

you know, the CUTTING you left on yr desk top when I was waxing —
you know, that CRICKET which said you wasn't no good at all?

when you got TERRIBLE, stamping and raging calling him stupid
and how the man was a FOOL, which was the day you took DRINK.

'What is to one class of minds and perceptions exaggeration,
is to another plain truth' (Dickens remarks in a brief

preface to *Chuzzlewit*). 'I have not touched one character straight
from
life, but some counterpart of that very character has

asked me, incredulous, "Really now *did you* ever see, *really*,
anyone *really* like that?" ' (this is the gist, not precise).

Well I can tell that old cricket that this is JUST how we speaks like,
me and the Capting and all (only not just in two lines).

One time, returning to home port, fell in with Englishman (16-
gunner) bound England from Spain; hailed her heave-to and belay.

After a skirmish we forced her to strike her colours and seized her.
Auctioned her off at Rochelle; carried the prize to Bordeaux.

Our tars had been so long absent from home that now we indulged
in
every extravagant vice, ere we be called to ye Deep.

Merchants advanced us, without hesitation, money and goods on
promise of that which was our share of the booty, d'ye see?

We spent the night in whatever amusements best pleased our
fancy –
claret and gore and the stench of ye rank pox-festered trulls.

We spent the next day traversing the town in masquerade, ranting,
had ourselves carried in chairs, lighted with torches, at noon.

As we caroused thus abroad we caused music, plucked forth from
gambas
boldly, t'embellish the raw, rude Dionysian debauch.

And the drear consequence of this gross wanton mass
indiscretion
was the untimely demise of damned near all the whole crew.

Jimmy 'The Beard' Ferrozzo, aged 40, Manager of the
Condor Club, where I now work (down San Francisco's North
Beach),

died when the stage-prop piano we use for Carol the stripper
pinned him tight into the roof, causing his breathing to stop.

Mr Boyd Stephens, the medical guy who did the autopsy,
said that Ferrozzo was pressed so tight he couldn't inhale,

said that 'Compression Asphyxia' is the name of the ball-game–
pressure had squashed up the chest so hard it couldn't expand.

I have been Caretaker down at the topless Condor Club now for,
must be a couple of years. When I unlocked, 9 a.m.,

I found Ferrozzo draped over his girlfriend (23-year-old
Trixie – this slag from the Club, nude Go-Go dancer, you know?).

She had no clothes on and she was stuck, screaming, under him – it
was
three hours before she could be freed by the cops from the raised

Steinway, a prop they have used at the Club for 2 decades almost
(topless star Carol descends, sprawled on the keys, to the stage).

Even now, no one knows what caused the joke piano to rise up
into the ceiling, 12 ft., pinning Ferrozzo and Trix.

Police say the motor that operates on the lifting device had
burned out and couldn't be switched so as to bring it back down.

Some way the Manager's body had kept her 2 or 3 inches
off of the ceiling and stopped Trixie herself being crushed.

Det. Whitney Gunther says: 'She was so drunk she doesn't
remember
laying down nude on the strings inside the grand – she just knows

sometime that a.m. she woke up to hear the twanging of taut wires.'
Man! What an Exit, you know? Welter of plucked gut and spunk.

Only, because it has broke (I.T.V.) we HAD to watch 'Seasars' –
stories about the roam Kings, dirty disgusting old lot.

One of them dressed up in smelly old skins and rushed out at captives
wounding there PRIVATES with KNIFE. also had LOVED his own Mam.

this is called 'Narrow' which plays on a fiddle, all the time Roam burnd
but why it Brakes is because, my man has FIXED it last week

Also my mack is at cleaners because of kiddies which MARK it
ever so bad with their spit. They should be children of Roam —

what with the way they go on with their dirty, horrible, habbits
One of which made them all HEAR while he plays music all nite.

This one is known as 'Callegulum' which is v. funny name for
King but is THERE on t.v. So must be right. It is pink

leather effect with a belt and the reason why there is broken
glass on Barometer is: cutting a LONG story short.

My man is playing it just as a banjo, being the SAME SHAPE,
singing the George Formby Song. and he has drop it on FLOOR

SO that the glass and the silvery stuff you get in it all come
out and can not be got back. One of them SAWED men in half

also he has a poor soul stabbed to death with terrible pen nibs
also a mans' brains flogged out using a CHAIN for three days

which is the same sort of thing that you get in newspaper these days.
what with the Irish and that, so I have bought a new GAMP.

That is because of the Mack but he also made FATHER's go to
SEE their own kiddies killed dead, that was the worst thing of all

so it has broke and the needle now <u>ALWAYS</u> points to the STORMY –
he is a fool to have PLAYED (Formby) But ROAM is BAD TIME

Nero springs out girt in lynx pelts and slits slave's dick with a
razor . . .

ROAM is BAD TIME, as is Wolves: January '84,

19-year-olds Brian Johnson and friend Troy Blakeway are jogging,
that they may catch the last bus, after a disco in town.

Leaving the Old Vic Hotel, Wolverhampton, they are pursued by
25 rampaging youths (West Indians, it appears).

Johnson leaps onto a bus but is stabbed twice just as the doors close
(two deep long cuts in the thigh, 15 and 12 inches long).

At the Royal Hospital he receives more than seventy stitches.
Blakeway is knifed in the back, trying to flee from the mob –

in the deep 6-inch-long gash he gets thirty stitches; a sobbing
middle-aged parent attends (whose hand a nurse gently pats).

'Very sharp instruments must have been used for making these
nasty
injuries' C.I.D. says (Johnson and Blakeway concur).

It has not been without usefulness that the Press has administered
wholesale mad slovenly filth, glibly in apposite prose,

for it has wholly anaesthetized us to what we would either
break under horror of, or, join in, encouraged by trends.

Horrible headlines don't penetrate. Pongoid crania carry
on as though nothing were wrong. *Homo autophagous*, Inc.

Gillian Weaver aged 22 walking 4-year-old daughter
home when a girl and three men – hang on, this isn't just *news:*

Gillian Weaver aged 22 walking 4-year-old daughter
home when a girl and three men push her to pavement and steal

£3 from purse – she sits weeping and nursing 4-year-old (let's not
wax sentimental re kids; let's stick to facts, here *are* facts).

As she sits weeping and hugging her daughter, one of the muggers
comes back and razors her thus **slashes her face 50 times**

(this is the Mirror and not my*self* – *I* have no axe to grind, right?)
C.I.D. seeks three blacks plus one spotty, ginger-haired white.

Meanwhile, I've gotten the *5-minute Uke Course* (Guaranteed
Foolproof) –
plinkplinka plinkplinka plonk plinkplinka plinkplinka plonk.

Maybe we're better off under the Civic Centre than up there
what with the LUTEing and that – them inner-cities is BAD,

maybe we're better off here in his WRITINGS, orrible though they
often is sometimes, than THERE – out in that awful real-life

what with its madness and sometimes I thinks the Capting's the only
sane one among the whole lot – Four or five leagues West-sou'west!

Steadily bear away under a reefed lug foresail, ye bilge rats,
synne rises firey and red – sure indycation o' gales,

we have entrapped us a sea-mew and served the blood to ye
                                                      weakest
members of crew, and myself? Liver and heart and ye guts.

For accompanying singing, the haunting harmony of the Uke has no
superior! Soft summer nights and the Uke are inseparable pals! To
wintery jollities the Uke adds zip and sparkle! Too much mystery
and confusion have shrouded Uke playing! The Uke is an instru-
ment for the best accompanying of happytime songs! Beautiful and
very unusual effects can be achieved! <u>You</u> can learn to play richly
harmonious accompaniments *in only a few minutes* by this New
Method, and when you have done that **you have accomplished a
great deal!**

'This is not Poetry, this is reality, untreated, nasty',
'This is demotic and cheap', 'This is mere caricature',

'This is just relishing violent, nasty . . .' so on and so forth,
Grub St. reviewing its own lame valedictory tosh –

Don't you go brooding and brooding and getting all of a state sir
just cos the LITARY GENT don't seem to like your nice books.

Like the old man used to always say 'When we wants YOU to chirp-up,
matey, we'll rattle the cage' – don't heed their old tommy-rot.

212

Grasp the pick lightly between thumb and first finger of right hand.
Do not pinch! Move tip of pick back and forth across all four strings.
Let that wrist hang loose! Start slow and then increase speed until
you produce a smooth, even tone. Well done! The speed you move
the pick across the strings will depend on what we call *tempo* (that
means *time*) of the number you're accompanying! Well done! **That
sounds just dandy!**

These are the questions that Councillors mean to raise at the
Meeting:
how much promethium remains? Has there been tritium used?

Why did the Army deny there was any contamination?
How do they mean to assure residents no risk remains?

What was the level of contamination? Where had it come from?
What is a 'low level' leak? Why was the public not told?

Why has the Army consistently issued flagrant denials
that any toxin remained after these secret 'events'?

Carrying on as though things were O.K. is what we are good at –
fall-out-proof bunkers are built, orbiting space stations planned.

*Only, it's worse in the papers than what you stick in your writings, what
with I seen a man knocked down WITH MY OWN EYES by black man and
poor soul that was muged was ON CRUTCHES and that is gospel truth but
not as bad as burning baby with CIG END which some swine done to get
purse from mother of two. So even if they are out of work it is NOT RIGHT
they should hurt their own townpeoples. Any road it is too late now so we
can just HOPE FOR BEST which I DO, and will only live in shelter or
outer spaces if there is no other possible. But will NOT eat sardines morning
noon and night.*

Finally now we return to the deep, and reaching our dim craft
drag her black hull through safe shale down to the fathomless brine.

Next, to the dark-bellied vessel we carry white sails and mainmast,
lifting aboard her the sheep, white tup and black ewe, and now,

heavily laden with misery, shedding tears in abundance,
hark to our skipper's command, nimble in wit and resource.

Thus we embark while astern of us rise up sail-swelling breezes
surging the blue-prowed ship forth, 12 knots with main-skysail set.

So, d'ye see, after putting our gear and tackle in order,
all we can do is observe, course set by helmsman and wind.

Thus with full canvas we traverse the waters into ye blackness;
tenebrose, fog-bound, the bar, into the tow of the stream.

Here is perpetual smoke of a city unpierced by sunlight
where ye Cimmerians dwell, unvisible from above.

Here we make fast and drive up from the bilges, bleating, the
                                                    stunned sheep
into these bunkers of lead, granite and greyness and stench.

Wend your luff, messmates, and let go the skysail halliards, mister,
cut the brace pennants and stays, reef the fore-topgallant in,

falling barometer, send down the skysail yard from aloft, sir,
strum with felt pick back and forth, lightly across all four strings,

all sail should be double-gasketted, stow the mainsail and crossjack,
make yr pentameters taut: two-and-a-half feet times two,

bend ye now three lower storm-staysails and a storm spanker, mister
take in the three upper tops, close-reef the foresail, F sharp,

tighten the B string and place finger at the back of the second
fret of the A string and keep spondees and dactyls close-clewed.

trim yr heroic hexameter (or it may be dactylic),
splice the pentameter aft, finger yr frets as ye go

surely we shouldn't be speaking like this sir, not in Allergic
Dis Talk, taint natural-like: I'm goin back to me prawse

only I've not been old self since they started the TREATMENT but do not
WORRY as they SWEAR it is non malingerent tumer ONLY which only in
my opinion only needs GOOD TONIC and will soon be old self again but
sometimes feeling bit on queer side that is to be expected the doctor say, but
what with one thing and another and the worry over eldest boy in trouble
with LAW I do not know which way to turn but I do wonder when you read
these cases what do the mothers think. and the father's. because they are all
some mothers children which loves them I should say. Even if they are vilent
crimnal. So will soon be back on feet again but this worry is worrying with
internashnal TROUBLE brewing as the BULLETIN says and I do not feel so
perky as previous. So will sign of for the present

I had believed myself fairly inured to foolishness after
6 months for Reuter's in parched mad bloody Lebanon, but

leaving the hotel that morning (with Dickie Pratt, of the Mirror),
in the main street of Sidon, I was presented with this:

out from the shade of the shelled former Admin. Offices stepped a
miniature, wielding a huge glinting black muzzle and stock,

just as a fat juicy jeep of Israelis swung into vision.
Three or four seconds he stood, sputtering hail at the jeep –

windscreen-glass frosted and one of the front seat occupants oozed
red,
there was a crackle of fire, ten or so seconds, and then,

as from a colander, into the pavement streamed out the juices
of the assailant, a slight soldier/homunculus. Well,

nobody looks for a *motive* from these Old Testament shitters –
thick hate is still in the genes. I learned the boy was aged 12.

Say! At the outset, the beginner may find his fingers just a little bit
stiff and clumsy but this disappears quickly after a little practice! So

215

why not keep right on along gut-pluck-a-plickin come rain or come shine! Yes *Sir*! Let's start with the **little finger down** where the neck joins the body . . .

'Tries to be shocking', 'Predictable, coarse, insensitive, tasteless
                                                                    . . .'
when I want you to chirp-up, matey, I'll rattle the cage.

What with the waiting and not knowing what on earth is the matter
up in the cities and that. Still, it was awful up there

what with last Wednesday that one what married him from the Top Flats
pushing the babby she was, down by the Preesint new shops,

suddenly found erself total surrounded by what-do-you-call-em?
them Rasterfastium blacks; you know, the ones with the LOCKS.

One got er purse but the pleece come and then the LEADER a FAT man
snatched up the babby and STABBED — right in the EYE with a pen,

animals that's what I think of them monsters horrible wild BEASTS
not safe to walk in the streets — not that we could NOW, of course

only it's funny for us being down here under the Civict
Centre – I thought it was all Underground Car Parks and that.

During this voyage ye heavens has been so dree overcast that
no observation by stars, nor yet by sun can be got.

Little round light like a tremulous faint star streams along sparking,
blazes blue, shoots shroud to shroud, running along ye mainyard,

stays half the night with us, settles on fore-shrouds. Spaniards call it
Fire of St. Elmo – be damned! Fire of ye Devil, it may be.

Only the Capting gets mixed up about his time in the Navy —
muddles it up with them YARNS. You know, them one what you READ,

not as I'm one for the books and that what with doing the housewort
(no Womans Libbance for ME, what with that much things to do.

get on with THIS Viv and THAT Viv and, well you has to LIVE don't you?
that's what I think, any road). Close-clew your sails, mates, avast,

shew a reefed foresail to steer by and run for harbour my buckoes,
oakum discharged from hull's seams; pipe up all hands to the
pumps!

Make ye now ready for Davy Jones, messmates, get ye the strings
tuned,
highest grade sheep's gut, they be – list to the boatman, belay,

as o'er the stream we glide borne by the rolling tide chanting and
rowing . . .
Place your 3rd finger behind 3rd fret of 4th string and strum

Only I've never been happy but what I'm pottering, I ain't —
always the pottering sort, that's why I hates coming DOWN

mind you the Powertree Bloke and the Capting doesn't arf GABBLE –
what with the Capting his YARNS: tother keeps chaingin is VOICE

anyone'd think they was Everyone All Times Everywhere, way they
gabbles and rambles and that: still, they can't help it, poor souls.

Whatsisname says to me 'Viv you're the life and soul of the party' —
Viv, he says, MEANS life, you know (in Greek or Lating or French)

p̄linkp̄linkǎ | p̄linkp̄linkǎ | p̄linkp̄linkǎ | p̄linkp̄link | p̄linkplinkǎ |
p̄linkp̄link
p̄linkp̄linkǎ | p̄linkp̄linkǎ | p̄lonk || p̄linkplinkǎ | p̄linkp̄linkǎ | p̄lonk

'Swear by Almighty . . . the evidence
I shall . . . and nothing but the . . .'
　'Sergeant Gillespie, please tell,
　in your own words, to the Court . . .'

'Constable Renton walked into the
charge room just a few moments
　after the time when Carliell
　had been allegedly punched

and he said "I'm sorry, Sarge, but I
caught him one with my ring like.
　Couldn't we sort something out?"
　I said "Get out of the room."

I said "I'm not putting my wife and
kids on the line for you, Renton."
　Carliell had been brought in drunk.'
　'Ladies and gentlemen of . . .

I submit that Mr Carliell was
struck a blow of such vicious . . .
　Call Mr Peter Lee . . . Now,
　you, on the night of . . . next cell . . .

tell the Court, please Mr Lee, what you
heard that night in the next cell.'
　'I could hear screaming, and he
　shouted "You've knocked out my eye.

Why have you done this?" he shouted, and
I could hear him like screaming . . .'
　'Constable Renton is charged,
　ladies and gentlemen of . . .'

*

['. . . you will not know me but . . . something in
common . . . both up at Oxford . . .
    six years your junior – yet
    both of us Balliol men!   ']

All of you goat-esses be not so
Frisky, lest the bold he-goat
    Rouseth himself to ye all!
    Muses, begin the sweet song.

['. . . so my dear Lockhart I venture to
send these "Lyrical Fragments
    Done into English" in case
    "Quarterly" readers may care . . .']

If 'tis your fancy to fasten your
Cloak-end on your right shoulder,
    And you can stand an attack,
    Get thee to Egypt forthwith.

We all grow grey at the temples and
Time's snow creeps down our cheek-bones;
    We should be active while sap
    Courses yet fresh in our joints.

['. . . Sir, I remain Yr. Obedient
Servant, Reverend Wolly,
    Parsonage, May '35,
    Claresmould-cum-Cowperly, Snotts.']

Eunica mocked me when I would have
Kissed her; then did she spit thrice
    Into her bosom and said
    'Neatherd, thy stench is obscene'.

*

In City Centre it were [you will
notice Regional Accent
    tweely denoted by quaint
    phrasing] me sister were there

visiting like, an er lad as is
nearly seven were took short –
    needed to go to the bog.
    Well, Public Toilets was near,

so er just took im along to em
but they couldn't use *Ladies*
    (where er could look arter im)
    cos there were queue like outside.

So er sends im in nex door like to
Gents as seemed to be empty.
    Well, e seemed gorn a long time;
    so, when some feller comes by,

er says Just take a look in please an
see if nipper's OK like.
    So this bloke goes in you know.
    Sudden-like, out runs three youths

– what they ad done were to stuff the kid's
mouth with bog-paper roll then
    cut with a penknife is poor
    little dick orf and is balls.

                    *

    [This isn't elegy but
    thanksgiving; therefore invert –
place the pentameter first and the
hymn/hexameter after.]

220

April – the Met. Office says
   warmest since records began.
Pure cerulean of sky and, be-
hind the cottage, thick-fleeced ewes

   suckle robust new Clun lambs,
      celandines gleam from sunned turf,
first of the season's *Phylloscopus*
warblers *hweet* from the pleached thorn,

   primrose – [enough of this crap.
   Sounds like the Plashy Fen School.
No *list* of species can ever be
more than gross insult to them –

   patronized tweely by bards
      (awfully keen on Wild Life)].
I shall confine myself merely to
bringing forth a scrubbed table,

   setting it down in lush grass,
      placing rich wallflowers, just cut,
fumous of uncloying honey, and
to the business of olives,

   watercress, paprika, rice,
      breaking moist pizza apart
(anchovies, capers and sharp oreg-
ano bruised into fragrance),

   sloshing out goblets of light
      sap-green cool Tokay d'Alsace,
cascading Vichy, bright sparkle of
glassfuls frosted to fjord-cold . . .

[All he could do was *report*
      horrible and (some) nice things.]
There is an impotent gratitude
goes with godless well-being.

     Elsewhere, the world is to-cock;
     here though, quite simply, this hour
glows as amongst the most joyful (old-
fashioned word) in a short life.

*

['There is a Madness abroad, and at home the
cities run bloody with Riot; my children,
know yourselves happy who, far from base Commerce,
plough your own acreage. Pray for all Statesmen.
Though we had nothing to do with them, we must
suffer for Sins of our sires . . .' My poor flock will
be unaware of Horatian echoes
when I deliver this to them on Sunday –
two or three scarcely forbearing to slumber.
There is a Madness abroad – in Retirement only, is Saneness.]

Sweet-voicèd holy-tongued maidens [quoth Alcman],
*My limbs can no longer carry me. Would that
I could go, be as the Kingfisher who doth
Go with his mates on the flower of the billow,
Height of foam having rejoicing heart sea-dark bird very sacred!*

[Far from the clash of arms, having the cure of
Claresmould-cum-Cowperly, all I can hope is
these humble fragments translated may lighten
some reader's heart, as my own is disburthened
daily engaging in, if futile, harmless
little unhurtful things. So, 'My Dear Lockhart . . .
whether the Lyrica Graeca here Englished
may be of interest to "Quarterly" readers . . .
Sir, I remain yr. most . . .' There is a Madness currently rampant.]

*Has been ordainèd three seasons, the Summer,
Winter, and Autumn the third one, and fourthly
Spring when things sprout or are lush but one can not,
You can not, it is not possible that one,
Eats to or feeds to satiety, fullness . . .
These words and song were invented, composed by,
Alcman-found, putting together the prolix,
Chattering noisiness utterance of some
Partridges . . .* [There is Madness abroad and elsewhere confusion.]

*

This is unclean: to eat turbots on Tuesdays,
tying the turban unclockwise at cockcrow,
cutting the beard in a south-facing mirror,
wearing the mitre whilst sipping the Bovril,
chawing the pig and the hen and the ox-tail,
kissing of crosses with peckers erected,
pinching of bottoms (except in a yashmak),
flapping of cocks at the star-spangled-banner,
snatching the claret-pot off of the vicar,
munching the wafer without genuflexion,
facing the East with the arse pointing backwards,
thinking of something a little bit risqué,
raising the cassock to show off the Y-fronts,
holding a Homburg without proper licence,
chewing the cud with another man's cattle,
groping the ladies – or gentry – o'Sundays,
leaving the tip on the old-plum-tree-shaker,
speaking in physics instead of the Claptrap,
failing to pay due obeisance to monkeys,
loving the platypus more than the True Duck,
death without Afterlife, smirking in Mecca,
laughing at funny hats, holding the tenet
how that the Word be but fucking baloney,
failing to laud the Accipiter which Our Lord saith is Wisdom.

Started by *Australopithecus,* these are
time-honoured Creeds (and all unHoly doubters
shall be enlightened by Pious Devices:
mayhems of tinytots, low flying hardwares,
kneecappings, letterbombs, deaths of the firstborns,
total extinctions of infidel unclean wrong-godded others).

*

[Letter to Lockhart. '. . . Alcmanium Metrum
may be of interest to "Quarterly" readers;
and I must hope that "The Scorpion" shall not
look with disfavour upon these slight, Englished,
little, unhurtful things. Sir, I remain yr . . .']

I know the Laws (or the musical modes or
Strains or the customs) of all of the winged tribe.

Ah, it is not Aphrodite but manic
Eros who plays at the games which a child will —
Caning a-down on the tips of the flowers,
Blooms of the sweet-smelling Cyperus *marsh plant;*
And do not, blooms of this, contact or touch me!

Peaks and the clefts of the mountains are sleeping,
Headlands and torrents, and crawling tribes (which are
Fed by the loamy black), animals of the
Mountain and race of the bees and the brute-beasts
Inside the deeps of the purple sea. They sleep
Also the tribes of extended attenuated or long-wings.

[Theme for the sermon at Claresmould o'Sunday:
'. . . visit the sins of the fathers upon the . . .
unto the third and the fourth generation . . .'
There is, odds-boddikins!, madness abroad, and
something horrendous seems likely to happen,
newspaper print blackens palms with the world's dirt,
Terrible Lizards* are being awoken –
daily the saurian monsters are raised and Genesis threatened.

All I can hope is for solace in these poor impotent strophes.]

*

There is a reciprocity here of maniac malice.
Theists are butchers, and twerpish their god-loves,
vicious PC punches prisoner's eye out,
Angels euphorically slaughter their buddies,
some PMs have Special Men to do-in your
Mrs or nipper or you if you vote wrong,

The nomenclature *Dinosauria* was established at the 1841 Plymouth meet-
ing of the British Association for the Advancement of Science.

kiddies are calling us cunts and will kill us,
addle-brained Counter-revs. maim all and sundry,
man sets to work on his neighbour with rip-saw,
horrified mum watches mugger stab tot blind,
niggers are here to be murdered in season,
OAP women are here to be fucked with lavatory brushes,
my little baby annoys me – I burn it, punch off the blisters.

[Bit of a habit, the feigned indignation,
various metres, Alcmanics and so forth,
ludic responses to global débâcles.
Just Going On remains possible through the
slick prestidigital art of Not Caring/Hopelessly Caring.]

                              *

[Yet I persist in this unhelpful habit,
sham, atavistic, unwanted, indulgent.
Thirty-four years since the death of John Lockhart . . . ,
still I can scarcely forbear to address him
(not that he printed my Lyrica Graeca
ever, alas, in his 'Quarterly' pages –
feeble Alcmanics I seem to recall then
proffering unto him . . . , equally weakly,
doubtless, these graspings at dignity through my
crude adaptation of Alcaeus' metric
into sad English beyond Elegiac . . .
In an old form is there dignity yet there?).
Ha! I am foundering, as is my Nation – Ocean o'erwhelms us.]

Now we must drunk and drink with a will we must,
Force or a zest since dead now is Myrsilus.
[Somehow I feel I have not captured
   quite what the beautiful fragment once was.

I have derived from Alcaeus' metrical
four-line invention; twisted to travesty,
   rudely reduced to dactyls, spondees,
      quantity ousted by Englished stressing.]

State of the four winds, I do not comprehend!
One wave is at us, rolling from gunwale there,
   One from the other, we in centre,
      Carried around in the black ship, hard pressed

By the great tempest; sea (or bilge) filling the
Hole for the mainmast; now all the sailcloth is
   Ragged with rent holes, holy, hole-rent,
      Great rips all over it, torn shards, sail-rips.

                              *

What are these birds come? Far from the (or from the
Bounds of the) Ocean? Dapple-necked, having-stripes,
   Tribe of the long-wings? [Long-wings, long-wings . . .
      Ah! But a tireful lacuna halts me.]

                              *

   [Garnering remnants, fossilized, civilized,
   I, mealy-mouthed disruptor of harmonies,
      strive in an old form (not strong, mayhap),
         cunningly structural – weakly helpful?]

Husband ye not one plant of the bushy tribe
First-before (or in) preference to the vine!
      [Sanity is a feeble weapon
         set against lunacy, nobly helpless.]